THE
FLIGHT

To Peter

With kind regards

Don Connor

THE STING OF
FLIGHT

DON W CONNOR

ATHENA PRESS LONDON

THE STING OF FLIGHT
Copyright © Don W Connor 2006

All Rights Reserved

No part of this book may be reproduced in any form
by photocopying or by any electronic or mechanical means,
including information storage or retrieval systems,
without permission in writing from both the copyright
owner and the publisher of this book.

ISBN 1 84401 671 4

First Published 2006 by
ATHENA PRESS
Queen's House, 2 Holly Road
Twickenham TW1 4EG
United Kingdom

Printed for Athena Press

Vultee Vengeance

Vultee Vengeance

Dedicated to my late wife, Joan.

Contents

I	Seeking Beyond	13
II	Growing Up	19
III	It's War	36
IV	Alone We Stand	51
V	The Conflict Widens	71
VI	Forwards and Backwards	91
VII	Up and Away	107
VIII	The Sting at Last	114
IX	The World at War	135
X	A Movement to India	161
XI	A Wing and a Prayer	194
XII	Home and the Final Phase	212

Climbing through the clean cold air,
Twisting, turning, dodging clouds,
Watching the pattern of fields below,
This is the sting of flight.

Pulling back the canopy,
Feeling the bite of wind on cheek,
The sudden roar of throbbing motor –
This is the sting of flight.

Reducing speed and turning earthwards
The feel of airflow over wings,
Speed cut back and almost pausing –
Gentle union –
This is the sting of flight.

DWC

Chapter One
SEEKING BEYOND

'There is, no doubt, more in heaven and earth than we humans will ever know in this life'. In order to get a tiny grasp of one's own broader existence it is fascinating initially to look backwards to one's forebears. A bit like an artist laying down a wash of colour before the painting begins. To do this I have to look back more than three quarters of a century in my own lifetime and then seek beyond.

My maternal grandfather I knew only slightly when, as a small boy, I would meet him with my mother when visiting an aunt. He would enter the room looking for something – see my mother and me and say a few short words of welcome – bend down and kiss my head with his walrus moustache, which felt like a moist mop on my head. He would then solemnly give me a half-crown (quite a lot in those days), and say 'Be a good boy' and be gone. He was a man of few words.

William Hendry was a Scot from Kirkudbright. He came south, married Elizabeth Cottrell, my grandmother, and built his adult life around the River Thames. He became a Thames pilot and his view must have included tall ships and sailing barges with rigging flapping in the breeze, and early steam-powered vessels waiting to discharge cargo in the London docks. His knowledge of the tides must have been considerable, covering the estuary and the river.

In his later years he became a shipwright and painter with artistic leanings. He was chosen to paint the interior design of Queen Victoria's state barge, which I understand had gold filigree decorations. My mother told me he was also the first man in his area to get motorised transport, in the form of a motorised bicycle. Eventually he formed a club, and a group of associates would dress up in their knickerbocker suits and ride out to the countryside at the weekend.

Towards the end of his life, in his eighties, my grandmother already dead, he was living with one of my aunts. He became bored, walked out of the house and went to the London Docks. He persuaded some painters to give him something to do. Very shortly afterwards he was over the side of a ship dangling in a cradle, from which he promptly fell out into the river below. They fished him out of the water with a nasty gash on his head. He was given treatment and sent home. True to form, he frequently pulled off the dressing covering his wound to examine the healing process, much to my aunt's concern.

A year or so later he kept to his room, resting quite a lot. A frequent visitor was an old friend, Mr Jarman, who would arrive dressed in the garb of the river – shiny peaked cap, blue jersey worn under a reefer coat. Together they would yarn about old times over a bottle of whisky. Eventually he passed away quite peacefully, from what I was told, and the stories about the river came to an end.

My maternal grandmother died at the age of fifty-nine, before I was born. She gave birth to eight children, five girls and three boys. One died prematurely in a household accident – a joyful little boy named Oscar, running around the piano, tripping up and hitting his head on the corner of same, bringing on a condition which medical science could not deal with in those days.

Another son, affectionately known as Harry, engaged to be married before joining the army in World War I, was killed in unusual circumstances. He was a machine-gunner who got separated in a retreat. Single-handed he captured a shell crater full of German soldiers taking cover, and for this action he was recommended for the Military Medal. This decoration came with a reward of two weeks' leave from the front back home. Unfortunately, there was confusion with soldiers' numbers, and numbers took preference over surnames. A complete stranger got the leave knowing he was not entitled to it.

In those two weeks Harry was killed in a German artillery barrage. Eventually the mistake was rectified and the decoration was awarded posthumously. In November 1958 I received a letter from an old lady, Florence Courtiour – Harry's fiancée. She had never married and wanted to find a home for his medal before she died – I still hold it to this day.

The other son in the family, William, was the uncle from the Hendry family I knew quite well. William had been in the Second Boer War as well as Harry's war and had been gassed. He saw the worst of trench warfare and survived. He became a school teacher but somehow he finished up working in the London Docks like his father, to the end of his life. It was from him that I learned of the horrors of trench warfare.

My mother, Jane Doris, was the youngest child in the Hendry family. When young she was called Janey, but in later years she was known as Doris by everyone, with the exception of one elder sister who continued to call her Janey for the rest of her life.

When quite small, following the death of her brother Oscar, little Janey became very sad and withdrawn as she missed her former playmate so much. A kind and thoughtful lady, who was a Sister of Mercy in their church and Sunday school, noticed how unhappy she had become for such a small child, and decided to help. She contacted her sister, Lady Hogg who lived in a large mansion, Berry Head House in Brixham, South Devon, suggesting that a holiday for little Janey away from her family would be beneficial. Very soon Janey was on her way for a holiday she would never forget.

Lady Hogg was in fact an invalid, as she had previously fallen from her horse and sustained a serious back injury. Most of the day she spent lying on a couch and could not do much for little Janey, but help was at hand. The housekeeper and servants joined in to amuse her and took her out for walks and showed her the beach and scenery. She must have been wide-eyed at her new surroundings and also found a new friend in a very intelligent collie dog.

She had noticed how a coastguard would take a short cut across an inlet of water by walking across the tops of some semi-submerged heavy wooden posts. Sometime later, out with her friends who were following, but just out of sight along a bendy coastline, little Janey decided to take the short cut across the posts. By now the collie was with her, probably wagging its tail. The coastguard's legs were longer than Janey's. She found that she needed a little jump to make each step. The inevitable happened – she fell in.

The water was deep and the current was fairly strong. Small girls of those days wore petticoats and dresses which puffed out around them. The result was that she floated like a large blossom on the water. The dog plunged into the water after her and grabbed a mouthful of her dress in its doggy jaws and swam around the inlet to the shallows of the beach before her clothes became waterlogged. An incredible story which my mother repeated on numerous occasions!

My grandmother, Elizabeth Hendry, was of Cornish stock. From descriptions and an old photograph, I know she was dark-haired, of medium height, very neat and efficient. She was religious and made all her children go to church and Sunday school. My mother and aunts all agreed that she worked continuously keeping them clean and well dressed, with the creases and pleats in their clothes all carefully pressed with a goffering iron, which had to be heated over the kitchen range. In fact she worked so hard at being a mother it shortened her life. The early 1900s was indeed a hard time for mothers.

My paternal grandfather, George Edward Cleeve Connor, who called himself Edward, was a story in himself on which Hollywood would have thrived. The Connor family was Irish and had a successful business in bloodstock. They were based in Dublin, but had several addresses. In those days horses were used for transportation as motor vehicles are used today. This was big business.

Edward became a barrister and practised in London. When he was around forty years old, upon the death of his father he inherited £40,000. In 1890 this would be the rough equivalent of £15 million at today's value. He left his chambers in London, married an innkeeper's daughter, Sarah by name, and sailed to America. Sarah was younger than Edward. Very little is known about their American adventure but they certainly made a hole in the inheritance. They also started a family.

Two sons, George and Percy, were born in America, and upon their return to England my own father, Walter was born, followed by Mabel, my favourite aunt. Sometime later one more baby David, arrived.

At this point, one can only speculate on what direction my grandfather's life was taking. He and his wife had squandered a large sum of money, and back in England his only plan was probably to try and get some support from his wealthy family. Apart from the Connor bloodstock side of the family, the name of Cleeve among his Christian names indicated another branch of the family which was involved in confectionery – at that time Cleeve's Toffees was a well known brand. There is no record of Edward's movements at that time, but it appears that his family cut him off. He was also apparently heavily in debt.

He may well have borrowed from his family in the first instance and they found there was no chance of repayment.

My father, Walter, and my aunt, Mabel, at the ages of approximately four and two respectively, were left outside a sweetshop by their mother, holding hands.

It was known that Sarah, their mother, had her new baby, David, in her arms and that she had virtually no money. It is also believed that the owners of the sweetshop probably knew or would have recognised the two little children holding hands. My father and aunt were brought up by kindly acquaintances and friends. In my father's case, in his teens he lived with his elder brother, George. As a young man he worked as a trainee in a fish and poulterer's shop and as soon as he was eighteen, in 1917, he joined the Royal Flying Corps, towards the end of World War I.

As for Sarah, my father's mother and my grandmother, the only record was by word of mouth. My aunt, Mabel, when a teenager, received a visit from her just once, and there the trail ran out.

My father's duties in the RFC, shortly to become the RAF, were mainly involved with aero-engines, and in the year following the end of the war, in 1919, he occasionally flew as an observing engineer, probably on air tests in the Vickers Vimmy – one of the first really successful twin-engined aircraft. The Vickers Vimmy was also one of the first serious record breakers for long distance flying in the aeronautical world.

My grandfather, Edward, died around the time I was born, in

1923, or just before. From family comments, I have concluded that although he must have been a waster, he could charm the birds off a tree and talk the hind leg off a donkey. He apparently died in a poor house of the times and was popular with the brethren within.

My father, Walter Connor, was a quiet, gentle person who never mentioned the sadness of his early life to me directly, but my mother and Aunt Mabel gradually unfolded the sad history to me over the years. There was an inbuilt sadness and possibly bitterness at being left alone in the world at an early age without a mother or father to turn to, although they were both alive somewhere at the time. As I grew older I appreciated he had a great deal of courage but his working life had taken the wrong path, and he deserved much better. His tragic childhood had robbed him of his true potential.

My mother was a kind and loyal person, and she believed that boys should be boys. She was a great encouragement to me and never tried to block my ideas. If she thought something was not quite right she would gently guide me in the right direction.

As a young woman she worked as a trainee milliner, and in later years would tell amusing stories about important customers. Ladies' hats at that time were an important fashion accessory, particularly amongst the well-to-do, and the airs and graces as the hats were tried on have made the background for many a comedy. One particular customer to visit my mother's department was a certain Lady Brook-Ridley, who would breeze into the shop and the staff would fall about themselves to keep her custom.

My mother met my father in 1919, when he came home on leave and they were staying in the same road.

Chapter Two
GROWING UP

After being demobilised from the RAF in 1922, my father found that life had again become a struggle, as jobs were few and far between. In those days there was no great demand for his expertise in aero-engines. He was now married to my mother and I was a twinkle on the horizon. In desperation he finally got a job driving a motor roller, as new roads and houses were being planned in Essex.

Together they lived in a house in Old Barking they shared with an engineer who had just returned from the Far East. The house was no more than a terraced cottage by today's standards, but it had three bedrooms. The engineer, Frank Stringer, eventually moved on. Both my parents referred to him in friendly terms. Before he left he gave them various pieces of equipment and a Chinese wooden trinket box with a carved lid (which survives in my possession to this day). They now had a complete home they could call their own.

Eventually, the job situation got worse as the motor roller requirement ground to a halt. My father was out of work again, which he never forgot. Then somehow he managed to get a job as a bus conductor.

In those days bus conductors dressed with military smartness. Family photographs show him in uniform wearing a white stiff winged collar and black tie. Buttons and badges on the uniform were polished with metal polish.

The bright red buses of the General Omnibus Company had a curving staircase at the back which was completely open to the elements. Initially the top deck was also open, but later a roof became a necessity and finally, when the company became the London Passenger Transport Board a closed staircase was added to a new model. The conductor was completely responsible for looking after the passengers and my father would help ladies, old people and children on and off the bus. In the days of heavy pea-soup fogs, he would often walk miles in front of the bus holding a lighted flare to guide the driver safely back to base.

During times of industrial unrest when virtually the whole force of drivers and conductors would refuse to work, he and possibly one other would be the only members who would walk through the picket line and report for work. He claimed that the bus crews who came out on strike did not deserve to have a job. Of course, amongst some of the striking committee tempers flared, and as a boy I remember he came home one day following a full return to work looking very troubled. He said that a driver had driven his bus straight at him when he was walking across the bus garage floor and he had to jump clear. I felt very sorry for him. He did nothing about it.

I was an only child, and I enjoyed a fairly untroubled existence, thanks to my hard-working parents. Our house was in a cul-de-sac named William Street. The small, neat houses in this street were all very similar, with little front gardens and adequate back gardens. Some had a tree in the front and others a privet hedge. Everyone seemed to be friendly. Most of these houses had been built around 1902 and a few in the late 1890s. Ours was one of the former type, which was slightly improved from the 1890s version but building standards had not changed much over the period.

At the end of this street was the back of a brick stable. All through the 1920s carthorses were still a common sight. These horses were fairly large and as a boy I can remember the noise they made stamping their hooves throughout the night.

When quite small, my father would occasionally obtain an empty orange box for firewood from a friendly greengrocer. I quickly realised that with a little imagination this orange box could be transformed into a racing car or an aeroplane. My father would be at the stage of removing nails protruding from the open side, before chopping up for firewood. I would intercept at this point with a cushion and a saucepan lid, and sit between the box divider to become a racing driver. Alternatively, my mother's copper stick would replace the saucepan lid and become the joystick of an aeroplane.

There was one particular incident, still clear in my memory, when I was about seven or eight years old. I was mugged (in modern parlance) on the way to Sunday school in the afternoon.

At the end of William Street, to one side of the stable, was an alleyway. This was a short cut to the world beyond. One side of the path was green with gardens – a pleasant enough sight, but on the other – horror of horrors was a crumbling wall which half hid the view of Back Reform Place. The name could not be more descriptive.

As I walked on my way to Sunday school, and so close to home, halfway along this alleyway several larger boys suddenly jumped out from an adjoining path from the garden side and surrounded me. They wanted money and I had my Sunday school subs in my pocket. They did not waste any time and the struggle was limited. They ran off faster than they had appeared.

I turned and went back home, feeling bad about losing the money and upset that I had not put up stiffer resistance, but in hindsight it was probably just as well. My father was in the house, and immediately I blurted out the story he rushed to the front door, and I remember trying to stop him, but I was too small. He surged out of the house to find the boys, but of course they had vanished, probably into the shadows of Back Reform Place. From that time onwards I was always very alert as I approached the adjoining path in the alleyway and only breathed easily when I reached the main road.

As a child I did not understand why there was so much difference in the way people lived, but in later years came to the understanding that lack of love, Christian ethics, money, education and ambition can drag human beings down into an underclass.

Life moved on. My mother was keen that I should maintain some religious education, although as a child I was not over pleased. In due course the Sunday school started to recruit boys for the church choir. Again my mother was keen on this. In later years it became obvious why this was so – her beloved brother Harry, who had been decorated and killed in World War I, had also been a choirboy and later a choirman.

To begin with I was somewhat self-conscious of wearing the cassock, surplice, white stiff collar and bow tie, but I liked the singing and the camaraderie of the other boys, and the full melody with the organ, male voices and two lady contraltos. A certain Mr Tarris was our choirmaster; he was responsible for building one of the best choirs in the area.

The Norman church of Saint Margaret, the Curfew Tower and the ruins of Barking Abbey are an enduring memory of my boyhood days. Added to this there was the church wolf-cub pack led by the excellent Mr Grinder who taught us many things and had a clever way of giving confidence in learning to swim. His trick was to offer sixpence for jumping into six feet of water towards him whilst he was treading water. Immediately I took up his challenge for sixpence and was surprised to find how quickly one gained the confidence to swim.

Some years later, I entered the model-making period of my boyhood. Schoolboys have always had an interest in aeroplanes, and a school friend, Dennis Watts, and I started to make small solid wooden aeroplanes from balsa wood. In those days there were no model kits and we copied the shapes from magazines. Dennis's models were always better than mine, as his father had the time to help him, and they would finish each model with four or five coats of lacquer, producing a gleaming finish.

One day my father showed me some old photographs from his days in the Royal Flying Corps and RAF. Amongst these were two photographs which really grabbed my attention. One was of the twin-engine Vickers Vimmy, with the crew proudly standing in the foreground, and the other of the remains of a crashed Avro after a bad landing. He also told me about different kinds of engines used in the early days, and how oil pressure was so vital. He described to me little-known facts about early aero-engines, where the rotary engine (not to be confused with a radial engine) completely revolved around the drive-shaft, and that in some early fighter planes the pilot had control only on either full power or idling through an 'on' or 'off' control. Hence the exciting 'brrr brrr' engine sound of planes as they came in to land, depicted in Hollywood films about World War I.

Apart from the subject of aeroplanes my father at the time

thought it a good idea to have a little dog around the place to take to the park. Very soon we acquired an intelligent half-breed dog named Jack, and during walks around the lake in the park the subject of fishing arose. I had already, two or three years earlier, trawled for tiddlers with a small net on the end of a cane, but now more serious stuff was the subject which involved rod and line.

The boating lake in the park did not hold fish large enough for the sport envisaged, so other waters became the subject of discussion. Eventually I became the proud owner of my first fishing rod, together with the miscellaneous items a young angler needed to enter the sport. It was all very exciting. We visited the odd lake farther afield where somewhat larger fish such as roach and gudgeon could be caught, and occasionally I even managed to make a catch myself. The fish were returned to the lake at the end of each venture.

Very soon, on one of the family visits to my father's sister, Aunt Mabel who lived in Tring, we discussed with some excitement the possibility of fishing in the old mill stream. Together with my father we found the old disused mill, and the very deep mill-pond close by, adjoining the stream. Without doubt, gazing into the mystical depth of this water at our feet for the first time, was for me a magical experience. It was crystal clear and very deep, and the largest wild freshwater fish I had ever seen were calmly swimming about. To one side of the pond, a jack pike, which had obviously already had its fill, was motionless in the water by the reeds with its next meal not far from its nose. (This peaceful and rare experience is still imbedded in my mind's eye a lifetime later.)

Soon my friend and I managed to get through the eleven plus scholarship, and we both went to the Park Modern School in Barking. A year or two later we were spreading our radius of cycling activity, being the only realistic low-cost method of transport for young lads. One of the high points was our first trip to Croydon Airport, which entailed a somewhat arduous journey across London. In those days the observation of 'Hercules' bi-plane airliners and the like landing and taking off was quite an experience, which impressed me greatly.

About this time the Park Modern School was at its zenith

under a firm and courageous headmaster, Mr Easterby. This school was a non fee-paying Selective Central School and was completely under the wing of the local council. It was one of the first co-educational schools. The girls sat on one side of the form-room and boys on the other. We were separated for some lessons such as science, art, handicraft and PT, and together for English, French, history, geography and mathematics.

The boys' game was rugby football, and the standards were high. The head, when well into his late fifties, would think nothing of demonstrating how to make a clean tackle. I was in Green House and my position was inside three-quarter. Unfortunately, there were several boys considered to be faster than me in other houses, so I could never quite get into the first team, but in our fourth year I was picked to be captain of the second team – a dubious entitlement. However, I enjoyed playing in the house games.

Running parallel to school activities I became interested in music. We had an old upright piano on which I would try to make music. Then for some reason I suddenly became aware of the haunting sound of the Hawaiian guitar – probably through the radio or films of the day – together with the bonus of the grass skirts of the female dancers.

I then discovered that a local academy of music, no more than five minutes walk from home, actually taught a whole range of stringed instruments, and the principal was a talented middle-aged lady, Miss Randall. She was a brilliant teacher. Approaching her academy one would hear, at different times, the strains of classical music played on the piano, violin and cello, the merry plucking of the long-scale banjo, the vibrating ripple of the mandolin and the melodious sounds of the guitar.

In those days fretted instruments were headed by an association called the BMG which stood for banjo, mandolin and guitar (would you believe). The BMG also promoted the production of musical arrangements for these three instruments, and sheet music could be purchased quite easily. Regrettably, the whole thing has changed in modern times. One hardly ever hears skilled playing of the long-scale banjo or mandolin, and the guitar has been slaughtered by over-electrification. These three instruments, played as they were intended, unamplified, can be a joy to the ear.

And so it was that I persuaded my parents to let me take up the Hawaiian steel guitar. The true Hawaiian guitar is the shape of a Spanish guitar but instead of pressing down the strings onto the frets with the fingers, one slides a piece of specially shaped steel along the metal strings over the frets. This produces the haunting strains of the South Sea islands. Also this style of playing stands up well when playing classical music, but with certain limitations. My first instrument was a fairly cheap affair, which Miss Randall organised for me. An advantage of the steel guitar is that one can make faster progress initially than the classical Spanish guitar, which uses some gut strings and also involves growing the fingernails of the plucking hand. Alternatively, there is the regular guitar which is played with fingers or plectrum instead of the fingernails, but this also needs a great deal of time initially and the tone is completely different. The steel guitar is played sitting down with the instrument across the knees, and best played with two finger picks and a thumb pick. I eventually reached the stage when I could play some unaccompanied solos, and Miss Randall decided I should apply for the first diploma – again which she organised. In due course I presented myself to John Alvey Turner in New Oxford Street and played my test piece. To my amazement I passed. My lessons continued and eventually I gained my second diploma.

Somehow, and I cannot remember why it came about, Miss Randall put my name forward to have an audition for young musicians to play in a BBC Children's Hour programme. It was at the time when things in Europe were looking distinctly unsettled, with civil war breaking out in Spain.

I can remember having the audition in a room completely on my own, and when I had finished playing a narrow curtain slid sideways, and behind a glass screen were the Children's Hour Broadcasting team, all sitting there nodding and smiling – but there was no sound – I was in a sealed studio. For a young person it was almost like a strange dream.

There was no end to this interlude – apparently some kind of reorganisation was going on in the BBC studios, which were being moved to another location. There was also more unrest in Europe. Not a word was received from the BBC. My musical career had ground to a halt – but not quite. Around this time I was a member of a local scout troop, and our scoutmaster, known by all as Charlie Chasmar, was a music teacher in a local school. Charlie wanted to produce a scout concert in St Margaret's Church Hall. For some unknown reason the theme was based around a prison. Charlie wrote the songs and music for this epic and the theme song was 'Twenty years behind the prison bars'. A large character with a face resembling a prize fighter was suddenly produced to sing this song – Charlie had some strange contacts. This lead singer, with a base voice, and a scout chorus in the background, would launch into:

> Twenty years behind the prison bars
> Twenty years away from home
> For twenty years I've never seen me missus or me kids
> It's a wonder I'm not dotty in the dome
> The world outside is so full of life
> But I'd rather stay indoors
> All I want is to see my wife
> And the kiddies whose daddy is gone
> Twenty years behind…

Suddenly I had a part in this epic. Charlie did not waste the slightest bit of talent. I had to play the Hawaiian guitar seated on a boulder in the corner of the stage dressed in convict's clothes complete with arrows, and the chosen peace of music from my repertoire was called 'Blue Lagoon'! Looking back on this episode I can only imagine the audience left the hall at the end of the show in a state of complete bewilderment.

When World War II commenced in September 1939, Charlie Chasmar, with his rather thick spectacles, was one of the first to volunteer as an air-gunner in the RAF. Because of his rather sub-standard eyesight he was given corrective flying goggles, and eventually after some training started flying as a tail gunner in one of the early bombers. He was killed almost immediately – poor Charlie, he didn't stand a chance.

Returning to my school activities, by 1938 Adolf Hitler was making some uncomfortable noises on the continent, but our housemaster, PT instructor and camping-club master, Mr James – much younger than the head – was well advanced in booking a twelve-day trip to the Continent. Initially, the idea had been to go to France as we were learning the French language, but with typical British thinking the decision was made to go to Germany, as it was much cheaper!

On 2 April 1938 at 8.30 a.m. we assembled at Barking Railway Station for the first leg of our journey. Our parents, with anxious faces, were also there to bid us a safe journey. The problem on their minds was the antics of Adolf Hitler, as already the daily newspapers were making some disparaging remarks about his activities.

Our journey took the school party to Victoria Station and thence to Dover on the Continental Express, arriving at 11.20 a.m. (not bad for those days). We immediately boarded the *Prince Leopold* channel steamer for the short voyage to Ostend. The sea was very calm and we all started eating, as schoolboys do at the least opportunity.

We had been instructed to keep a diary of events, and notes were taken of the slightest thing of interest – passed the midway lightship at 1.25 p.m. – a young German student played his saxophone, to our delight – we listened to the Oxford and Cambridge boat race on the radio in the saloon. It was all very civilised.

We eventually arrived in Ostend and found our train. Luggage was left on the train and all went off for a short walk, buying chocolate.

Our train journey eventually took us through the German frontier at Aachen, where we were boarded by custom officials who had a good look around. This was peacetime, so-called, but there were many German soldiers about. We became conscious that this was a different situation to that left behind back home.

And so we arrived in Cologne late in the evening and were greeted by two German students and our guide, and thence to our first youth hostel – everything highly organised.

Every night we stayed in a youth hostel and rose early 6.30–

7 a.m. We were always accompanied by Willi, our guide (a good-natured German who took no offence about our schoolboy jokes about the Nazis and their 'Heil Hitler' salute). In fact he almost joined in the fun. Sometimes and additionally two German girl students accompanied our excursions to various places of interest. Looking back, this was possibly all part of the Nazi propaganda to show how normal Germany was at the time, to encourage other school parties to make their visits to Nazi Germany.

Our own two masters with us, Mr James and Mr Bernard, kept things moving. At one point, in a Nazi youth hostel, we showed our German friends how fit we British were by building a human pyramid – one of Mr James's specialities from our PT sessions back home.

In Cologne Cathedral, we noted the large German swastika flags hanging around the inside against the walls, making a formidable Nazi display, which made us feel uncomfortable.

We visited Cologne Museum and various other places of interest. The tour proceeded in an organised manner, making the most of each day. In Bonn we visited Münster Monastery and the university. Then we covered Beethoven's House and saw the instruments he had actually played (plenty of culture shown to young visitors). We sang songs with German boys and girls. We took a tramcar to the Drachenfels and then hiked for miles and miles.

On another day we visited a brewery which made a famous lager deep down below ground level where the temperature was one degree below zero – all part of a special process. We were led down winding stone steps to where the vats of brewing lager were situated, and warned that all sandwiches were strictly *verboten* as a boy in a previous school party had leaned over a vat and dropped his sandwich within – the whole of the contents of this very special lager had been ruined!

After the brewery we hiked on and eventually we reached Maria Lache Monastery and listened to the monks singing mass. We had some lunch in a small hotel nearby, and then returned to be shown over the monastery by a monk. Then followed a long hike back to the railway station to catch a train to Koblenz and our hostel.

The next day we visited Kaiser Wilhelm's memorial. The shops were orderly and interesting. Later we visited a fortress on the right bank of the Rhine by walking over a pontoon bridge. We then discovered that the Germans also ate fish and chips, which we were quick to enjoy for our evening meal. We were surprised to find that in these parts the fish for frying was trout!

Our journey then took an interesting turn when we boarded a Rhine steamer for Bacharach and had a cooked lunch on board, which was much appreciated. The views along the Rhine at that time are a lasting memory, with the occasional picturesque castle jutting out into the water.

We arrived in Bacharach and hiked up a hill to our hostel, which in this case resembled a fortification. (In later years during the war, it could quite easily have become a stalag.) We were amazed to see so many sentry boxes about in these parts, and German soldiers wearing steel helmets. We all calmly went for a walk and admired the peaceful scenery.

The next day, 9 April, we hiked through Rhine forests and villages and played a game often performed by Boy Scouts called 'taking the flag'. As if to confirm some ominous event was about to take place, that same evening Adolf Hitler broadcast a speech to the German nation which lasted a very long time. We were advised to stay in the hostel. Some of us walked around the battlements of this castle-like building. From this vantage point we could view the surrounding area. Not a single person could be seen in whichever direction we looked. Every German was indoors with ears glued to the radio. We discovered later that this must have been propaganda concerning Hitler's recent move into Austria and how much the Nazis had achieved.

Looking back to these times, I am amazed that our school party was hardly conscious of what was going on in the background.

The following day, a visit to Bingen by the Rhine boat *Siegfried* was planned, and we later took a train to Frankfurt, where we found our hostel.

In the morning yet another cathedral was on the agenda, and the 300 steps climbed to the highest point gave us a wonderful view of the city. We then came down to earth and immediately visited a famous open-air sausage shop, but alas there was no time for sampling the products. There is one thing the Germans do really well and that is make a huge variety of succulent sausages – the propaganda machine really slipped up here if they wanted to impress a party of schoolboys! Following the sausage shop we visited an art gallery, and then suddenly stopped for lunch in Frankfurt University. In the afternoon we were taken to see the Graph Zeppelin House (as it was called), and then conducted over the Zeppelin – quite an experience. We returned to our hostel for dinner and a good night's sleep.

On 12 April we had a free morning, lunched in the hostel and then commenced our train journey homewards. First stop was Cologne, where we had dinner in a hotel. There we met some seasoned airmen from the Luftwaffe. This was quite by accident. We boys were all in our fifteenth year, whereas the Germans were probably in their forties and some were old enough to have been in World War I. Indeed they were as old as our fathers. They were all in uniform and their manner was jocular. One of the boys chirped up 'His father was in the Royal Flying Corps' – pointing at me. I was not quite sure where this left me, but the older of the Germans nodded, gave me a fairly stiff smile and said something like 'Ah! So,' which is what Germans say when they are not sure of the situation themselves. Our train journey then continued with sleeping and a meal. Night merged into day as we arrived in Brussels at daybreak – another schoolboy snack, then we ultimately arrived in Ostend at 8 a.m., followed by breakfast in a Belgian hotel, a walk along the beach and thence to the Channel port.

Most boys ate too many Belgian chocolate bars and felt a bit queasy on the return Channel crossing.

We came ashore in Dover at 2.34 p.m., on the 13 April and finally arrived home in the early evening.

Looking back on these notes one can see immediately that the Nazis used every situation to give the impression of culture, by carefully orchestrating tours through youth hostels for young people, and taking them only to carefully vetted places of interest. They could not, however, avoid us seeing the large number of German soldiers in uniform in the various places and railway stations we passed through. The atmosphere was totally different when we arrived back in the UK, at that time, which only goes to prove how unready we were for what followed.

We returned to school after our German adventure, a little more worldly for the experience and with the feeling that some kind of European crisis was building up.

We worked hard studying for the remainder of the school term into the summer months, and we learned that changes were taking place at the end of the term. Our school fourth year examination would be final. In previous years it was possible to stay on for a fifth year but alas the school was being shut down and a much larger school was being built some distance away. Our old school, with its two green quadrangles, would be no more. It was a disappointment to many people, including masters and mistresses. The headmaster would retire, and an excellent educational format would be changed.

Our leaving examination was taken, which was set by the local authority and was accepted as the equivalent to the School Certificate. I was never one of the top pupils but I surprised myself by getting the highest overall average mark based on all subjects – a dubious Jack-of-all-trades status!

Towards the end of 1938 storm clouds were gathering, but on 30 September, Neville Chamberlain, the British Prime Minister, met Adolf Hitler in his flat in Munich, following an earlier meeting that same day of the European big four – Britain, France, Germany and Italy – aimed at avoiding the outbreak of war. Whilst the statesmen were waiting for the experts to draw up the document, Chamberlain asked Hitler if he would care to have a private talk. Apparently Hitler jumped at the chance, hence the meeting in Hitler's private flat. The only other person present was the interpreter. Chamberlain produced a draft declaration which he had prepared specifically between the German Führer and Chancellor and the British Prime Minister, stating in so many words that the agreement drawn up a few hours earlier, plus the Anglo–German Naval Agreement, was symbolic of the fact that Germany and Britain would never go to war again, and together they would discuss any problems which might arise – thus assuring the peace of Europe, etc., etc.

Hitler signed Chamberlain's note without raising any objections. In due course Chamberlain arrived back at Heston Airport with the jointly signed declaration which he claimed was 'Peace in our time'. (Alas, as history showed us, the words of Hitler could not be trusted.)

My immediate personal problem was to earn some money and further my education. It seemed that war had been averted and we could all settle down to a peaceful existence.

In my final year at school I had opted for a commercial background which covered some elementary typing and shorthand. I had no intention of becoming a shorthand typist, but it was useful knowledge in those days of office work.

Eventually I applied to a private employment agency and they came up with an office junior's opportunity in the City of London, which sounded interesting. In those days, if one secured the job you then paid the agency for their services, which was reasonable. In due course I went along for an interview and was accepted.

The company's name was Rappings Limited (without a 'W'), and the office was in a rickety old building in Bond Court, Walbrook – situated some way behind the Mansion House. The business revolved around food wrapping, specialising in butter and margarine wrappers. The paper used for this purpose, in those far off days, was pure vegetable parchment, a high quality paper with somewhat amazing characteristics – if one digs deep enough it will be found this was originally a German-formulated paper – clever fellows, these Germans!

In modern times, staff working in offices go off to a gym to keep fit, pitching body and mind against all kinds of expensive apparatus. In 1938 office juniors in Rappings Limited had no need of this. There was no lift, only a narrow winding staircase which an office junior would be required to run up and down numerous times each day. First thing in the morning enormous metal-bound ledgers and other books had to be retrieved from the safe, which was located in a vault deep down in the basement of the building. Last thing at the end of the day, this process was of course reversed, followed by piles of post which had to be franked and delivered to the Post Office.

There was one character I shall never forget. He held the exalted position of company secretary. A middle-aged well-nourished fellow with large bushy eyebrows, he smoked a large briar pipe throughout the day which jutted from his jaw and was only removed when he spoke, which was in crisp commands. His office was on the second floor, was oak-panelled and very small – just large enough for his desk and hat and coatstand.

One of his specialities was to phone down to the general office, where five staff were located, including juniors at several levels, and command the petty cash clerk to send up a boy with a penny ha'penny adhesive stamp – he never held such trivia in his own office.

The first time this vital duty fell to me, I was warned that I should knock and await the command to enter. I skipped up the stairs, knocked on the door and awaited the response, which I thought I heard, and walked in with the penny ha'penny adhesive stamp slightly stuck to my fingers. I was confronted with the *Financial Times* widely spread open above the desk, with a podgy hand at each edge of the paper and a great column of tobacco smoke puffing upwards. The *FT* was lowered slowly, revealing bushy eyebrows and smoking pipe, and as one half of the paper collapsed as the pipe was removed for speech came the steady command, 'In future wait outside until I tell you to enter!' This I believed I had already done, but he had obviously decided to make his status clearly known to the new boy. I deposited the now tacky stamp on his blotting pad and withdrew.

Various office jobs were given me and gradually I fell into the routine of things. From time to time urgent outside city errands entered my sphere of activities, which included taking bills of lading along to a shipping office. Sometimes urgent entries had to be lodged in the custom house.

Another side of the business was printing, as every brand of butter or margarine required a printed design. This side of the business was quite interesting as artwork was required to produce the master plates of the design. A printing works in Southwark was a subsidiary of the organisation and daily communications and frequent visits became necessary.

The overall office atmosphere in Bond Court was a happy

one, apart from the pomp which was generated from the small oak-panelled office on the second floor. The directors, office managers and their secretaries were a pleasant lot and spread over the first and second floors.

On the ground floor was the accounts department where the huge metal-bound ledgers were in daily use by three male bookkeepers sitting on high stools, with the chief accountant sitting on a chair at his desk – the latter being a mostly jovial quaint Dickensian character, which matched the rickety building. He was short in stature and proportionately rather wide and could never quite get my first name right – I would be called Desmond or David, but never Donald. When the tea lady arrived our friendly accountant would move into his favourite rhyme: 'Here we are so merry and so free. Here comes Mrs Hill with the tea' – the freedom directly referring to the gymnastics of Adolf Hitler in Europe.

Life moved on, developing into a steady routine at work. I decided I would buy myself a better Hawaiian guitar and together with my father and mother I visited a famous musical instrument shop, Clifford Essex in Shaftesbury Avenue. A specially shaped instrument for the method of playing was chosen, and the tone was a vast improvement on my first instrument – for me it was an exciting experience.

My numerous promenades along Leadenhall Street and surrounding areas brought me past the odd shop front interspersed between office blocks. In those days almost everybody smoked tobacco in its various forms. A number of these shops had windows displaying great pyramid mounds of finest golden Virginian tobacco, described as being cool and mellow.

With everybody around me smoking cigarettes, pipes and cigars I decided it was time for me to enter the pipe brigade and try this cool and mellow experience, which I did. I had already smoked an occasional cigarette, and I felt that the pipe was more worldly, and the tapping out of the dead tobacco on the heel of the shoe gave a certain *je ne sais quoi*.

Alas, I discovered that this smoking of the pipe was not all it was cracked up to be, but I felt I must persevere to keep face with the rest of the chaps in the city. Indeed the worldly unwise were saying it was just a matter of time before I acquired the taste and one could always return to the cigarette until one developed the taste for pipe tobacco. It is amazing how often mankind has been so easily led into unhealthy habits and situations throughout history. After all, the tobacco habit dated from the time when Sir Walter Raleigh brought back a small shipment of dried leaves from the American Indians and demonstrated how to obtain the aroma by setting fire to them in various ways, then sucking in the smoke through the mouth. A questionable performance, but oh boy how this caught on!

Word filtered through that my old school, now in a new so-called modern building, was running a dance for old pupils on a certain Saturday evening. It was a cold winter's evening so I wore my newly acquired tweed overcoat. I invited one of the staff from Rappings' general office, a couple of years my senior. He was keen to bring along his new girlfriend. All went well, but when the dance finished we went to the cloakroom to collect our coats and to my dismay my new tweed coat had vanished. Faith in human nature took a jolt – I shivered all the way home!

As 1939 progressed the overall political situation was deteriorating sharply. I was taking evening classes in the SE Essex Polytechnic to further my office status. Work at the office continued and there was no let-up. Business was good and I had a couple of small rises in pay, but everyone was talking about the possibility of international problems becoming much worse.

Chapter Three
IT'S WAR

It became obvious that Hitler's ambition was to expand eastwards and his next plan was to invade Czechoslovakia. His initial excuse was to help the German nationals living in the bordering Sudetenland regions, but he had no intention of stopping at the border.

Chamberlain tried at every turn of event to stop war breaking out. Sometime later even Hitler's close ally Mussolini (who had previously plunged the Italian nation into war in Abyssinia and also got involved in the Spanish Civil War) tried to hold him back. The Italians were not ready for another war on a large scale involving Britain and France. The Duce was beginning to get cold feet, but did not wish to appear unsupportive towards the Führer's master plan. Hitler pressed on regardless with his overall expansion programme, making excuse after excuse and lying through his teeth.

The Czechs are a cultured race. They had a strong army and a large armaments potential centred on their Skoda works, but Hitler seemed to have enormous luck the way the cards were stacked and he took full advantage of the fact that the British and French desperately wanted peace, almost at any price. As if being led by the Devil himself, he proceeded with threats and diplomatic negotiations which fell into his lap.

14 March 1939 – German troop movements in Austria signal their entry into Czechoslovakia almost immediately. On the 15th, the occupation of Bohemia by the German army began at 6 a.m. It was not long before they had grabbed the Skoda works, giving Hitler a boost to his armament supply. The Czechs had been told by their leaders not to resist the invader. Again Hitler had managed to take over a small country by threats and cunning diplomacy. Two other nations, Hungary backed by Poland, took

advantage of the situation and grabbed a small chunk of Czech territory themselves, somewhat thoughtlessly. It would not be long before Poland would be ravaged herself.

It was clear that Hitler's next move would be to invade Poland, as he was making all kinds of threats in that direction. There followed more diplomatic activity throughout Europe with Britain and France stating they would stand by Poland if she were attacked. Enough was enough – the situation was clear-cut and Hitler had been formally advised.

On 22 August Germany negotiated a non-aggression pact with the Soviet Union. This suited both Germany and Russia, although their leaders hated each other. Not good news for Britain and France, as a threat from Russia in any form towards Germany would slow down Hitler's plans for expansion.

Around 23 August things started to hot up. The British government was alerted and took immediate action concerning the defence of coastal regions and deployed anti-aircraft defences for radar stations and other vital areas. Reservists of the Air Force and Auxiliaries including Balloon Squadrons were called up. Special cables would be attached to the balloons, creating a severe hazard to aircraft flying below the balloon altitude.

In the City of London we started to think seriously about defences in case of air raids. Two of our bookkeepers on the ground floor of our Bond Court offices were suddenly occupied filling sand bags around the front of the building, stripped to the waste in the sunshine, displaying their manly torsos for the benefit of passing giggling office girls.

All over the country air raid precautions were being planned, with wardens trained to organise appropriate action if bombs should fall. Gas masks had been issued some time previously in case Hitler should resort to gas attacks. Anderson air raid shelters were available for erection, which needed some heavy digging in the garden. The floor level was below ground level, and earth was piled on top of the curved corrugated iron roof. I remember helping my father site our shelter and thinking how damp this was going to be if we stayed inside for a long period.

Around this time plans were being made to evacuate children away from areas likely to be targeted by German air raids. Some families were even thinking of sending their children as far away as America. The Greater London area was considered to be extremely vulnerable.

25 August – The British Government announces a formal treaty with Poland and confirms its support.

31 August – Hitler issues his first directive of war.

1 September – The German Army invades Poland at dawn. Hitler's excuse was that the German nationals living in Poland were being ill-treated and terrorised, mainly because of the British Treaty with Poland.

The Poles put up a brave resistance with outdated fighting techniques and a much smaller army. They could not withstand the strength of the German armoured columns. After a short time the enemy cut through the Polish lines like a knife through cheese. Hitler had already agreed a Russian share of Poland, and later the Soviet Army was to move up to its agreed line, and on the 29th September the Russo-German treaty partitioning Poland was formally agreed.

3 September – Neville Chamberlain, the British Prime Minister, announces in a radio broadcast to the Nation at 11.15 a.m. that Great Britain was already at war with Germany. It also stated that the British ultimatum had been given to Germany at 9.30 p.m. on 1 September, and was followed by a final ultimatum at 9 a.m. on 3 September.

Almost immediately, at the end of Chamberlain's radio broadcast, the first active air raid siren sounded, but this appeared to be a false alarm and everyone heaved a sigh of relief. Then followed a swift meeting at Westminster when the Prime Minister told Winston Churchill that he was offering him, once again, the post of First Lord of the Admiralty and also membership of the War Cabinet.

The British armed forces were already alerted, but the Army was experiencing a quiet phase. However, the Admiralty was thrust into a sea war at once, with German U-boats already in position to carry out attacks on our shipping. (It was fortunate that in 1938 Duff Cooper had resolutely pressed for the mobilisation of the Royal Navy, in spite of Mr Chamberlain's 'Peace in our time' declaration with Adolf Hitler.)

The RAF was engaged in coastal patrols and in giving help wherever it was needed, but plainly much thought was being given to the training of more pilots and aircrew generally.

3 September – At 9 p.m. the passenger liner *Athenia* outward bound to America, was torpedoed. Many lives were lost, including some American passengers. This action against an unarmed passenger ship caused worldwide condemnation. The German government then announced that Winston Churchill had arranged to have a bomb put on board the liner to jeopardise relations between Germany and America. Hitler always appeared to have a story ready in an attempt to blind the world of the truth.

This sinking by U-boat signalled the commencement of one of the most deadly aspects of the sea war. On 14 October a daring attack was made by U-47, which crept into Scapa Flow and sank the battleship *Royal Oak* at anchor – a surprise attack thought to be impossible.

At sea there was much activity. Many merchant ships were attacked by U-boats and many lives were lost. Before the year ended one of the greatest Royal Navy actions against a powerful adversary, namely the German pocket battleship *Graf Spee*, took place, often referred to as the Battle of the River Plate. It finally ended off the coast of Montevideo, when, hopelessly trapped by the Royal Navy, the *Graf Spee*'s Captain Langsdorff decided to destroy his ship rather than make a run for it. The ship blew herself up and later Langsdorff shot himself. The spotter aircraft from the British cruiser *Ajax* witnessed the explosion.

In the earlier engagement, lives were lost on both sides. The *Graf Spee*, with her 11-inch guns and greater range inflicted considerable damage to three of our light cruisers, namely the *Exeter* with her 8-inch guns, and the *Ajax* and *Achilles* with only 6-inch guns.

The *Exeter* fought an extremely brave engagement in the encounter, hitting the German ship with her 8-inch guns almost immediately when both ships were approaching each other at full speed. The other two cruisers also made hits from different angles, but the heavier guns of the *Graf Spee* badly damaged the *Exeter* and she had to withdraw to make repairs and attend to her casualties. Sixty of her officers and men were killed and twenty wounded. The other two British cruisers making hits on the German ship also sustained damage, but it was their combined effect which made the German captain make a run for Montevideo with his very powerful heavily armoured vessel.

One cannot help but have a sneaking regard for the German Captain Langsdorff after the encounter as he made for Montevideo, a neutral port. There he could stay for a limited period and make repairs, land his wounded, see to his dead, and take on supplies. He also apparently transferred a large number of his crew to a German merchant ship. When his time ran out in the neutral port he had to move out, and on 17 December he decided to destroy his ship in the open sea, knowing that a powerful force of the Royal Navy was by now waiting for him. And so the first sea battle against a formidable surface raider ended, which was a considerable relief for our merchant ships already under threat from U-boats.

This, however, was not quite the end of the story, as the *Graf Spee*'s auxiliary vessel, the *Altmark*, was still at sea and was believed to have British prisoners on board previously captured from ships sunk by the *Graf Spee*. Ultimately, the *Altmark* was eventually cornered and boarded by the Royal Navy in a Norwegian fiord after a difficult situation with two Norwegian gunboat captains, who did not wish to upset Germany at this stage of their neutrality. Two hundred and ninety-nine prisoners were released from appalling conditions and returned home in British destroyers.

By now it was evident to all that the future was an unknown quantity. As for myself, work at Rappings Limited continued, with the older members of the male staff talking about conscription into one of the services. Over the years my parents and my Uncle Will had already given me some idea as to what could happen to individuals during a time of war, and my own father had been in the Royal Flying Corps. Therefore, my youthful mind had fixed on joining the RAF, but not yet, because I was too young. My thoughts revolved around the stories of trench warfare in World War I. This new war would be somewhat different, but I had already decided that if I became a fighter pilot I would be my own master up to a point, but this might be difficult to attain. However, it was worth a try.

I was told sometime later that the best way to get into flying with the RAF was to join the Air Training Corps and volunteer just before one reached the age of eighteen. So this was the route for me.

From now on the whole of Europe and part of Scandinavia were gradually being dragged into this terrible and wasteful conflict, started by Adolf Hitler and his Nazi hordes. The idea of war became infectious and early in December Russia suddenly got into a war with tiny Finland. Initially the Finns gave the Russian army a severe beating, but eventually the huge Soviet forces overwhelmed the brave Finns, who were finally forced into an armistice.

In the meantime, Hitler's Germany had continuously been building a vast arsenal of weapons for use with a very large mechanised army, together with large numbers of aircraft and a concentration of U-boats designed to sink our shipping and supplies so vital to our island home.

The tremendous weight of the German war machine was first felt in the strategic fighting in Norway where, in spite of the superior strength of the Royal Navy, we finally had to withdraw most of our forces because of Hitler's overwhelming air power. We had insufficient aircraft available to protect our capital ships and the troops clinging to vital positions in the Norwegian fiords, which the Germans badly needed. A number of Allied landings took place, including French Alpine troops, but eventually all were withdrawn. The Navy had, however, badly mauled the German Navy on a number of engagements.

Swedish iron ore was required continuously by Germany throughout summer and winter to maintain their vast war machine. During the summer months most shipments were sent through the Swedish port of Lulea in the Gulf of Bothnea, but in the winter months when this was frozen the route through Narvik on the west coast of Norway was Germany's solution. Hence the Allied attempt to slow down Hitler's armament production by cutting off his supply of iron ore.

The German plan of overrunning Norway also included Denmark in the first instance. Tiny Denmark, with its flat terrain, could do little to resist the enormous strength of the Nazi war machine. The air strikes against our shipping in the English Channel continued, with the RAF hitting back wherever possible. Hitler's war potential was getting stronger and stronger.

10 May – At last the Germans invade Holland and Belgium, which the Dutch had not expected. The British government is in crisis. Chamberlain resigns as Prime Minister, and within a few hours Winston Churchill takes the reigns and forms a new national coalition government.

Not long after, the German blitzkrieg was launched into France with such fury, using dive bombers ahead of a powerful highly mechanised army, that the speed of their advance had never been seen in history before. Despite the heroic resistance of the combined forces of the French, Belgian and the smaller British Expeditionary Force on different fronts, all in turn were forced to retreat, or be cut off.

27 May to 4 June 1940

Finally, British and French troops, with the help of RAF air cover, fought the German forces and held them just long enough to save a large part of our BEF and a small number of French troops. Eventually they were heroically picked from Dunkirk and the beaches by a flotilla of small British boats and ships, plus many destroyers, gunboats, minesweepers, trawlers, drifters, tugs and French and Belgian vessels in a continuous stream of activity. The whole time this remarkable action was underway, German artillery and dive bombers were doing their best to pound our soldiers into submission, but the evacuation was successful thanks to some heavy cloud cover, RAF fighters and a brave rearguard action by a small force who were prepared to sacrifice themselves in the last hours of the action if necessary. At the end of the day we still had enough trained soldiers returned intact to the safety of the UK, but without weapons or transport. All major equipment had to be left behind in order to evacuate our army quickly. These troops, and others in similar situations along the French coast, in the course of time would one day return to see Hitler's downfall.

Following Dunkirk, some days later, more British troops were cut off along the Havre peninsular, but later were safely embarked. Others in the St Valéry area were not so fortunate. Some delayed and confused French decisions, combined with a heavy sea fog, prevented the sea rescue taking place. This resulted in most of the 51st Highland Division becoming prisoners, after being trapped in the coastal region by overpowering enemy fire. The remainder of the BEF under General Brooke were given orders to withdraw, including the Canadian Division which had just come ashore and immediately returned to the ship which had brought them. The situation was hopeless, and it was important to get our soldiers back home with whatever equipment they had. These troops embarked for their homeward voyage from Brest, Cherbourg, St Malo and St Nazaire amidst heavy attacks from German aircraft.

There was one particularly horrifying incident which took place at St Nazaire when the liner *Lancastria* with 5,000 men on board was bombed as she was leaving. A fire broke out and burning fuel oil spread over the water. A bare 2,000 men survived.

The tremendous leadership of the British Prime Minister, Winston Churchill, with his uncanny insight into events, was a force which kept the nation on an even keel through these terrible times.

So far he had flown to France four times in a Flamingo aircraft, accompanied by up to three other members of the British government or armed forces, with twelve Hurricane fighters as escort each time, in order to meet the French leaders and to get an up-to-the-minute picture of the desperate battles raging. On the fourth such visit, on 11 June 1940, with Paris on the brink of being overrun by the enemy, they had to land the Flamingo on a remote airfield near Orleans whilst the French government departments were in the process of packing their bags to move to Tours. The high-level meeting took place in an old chateau in the vicinity of Briare near Orleans, with only one telephone, situated in the lavatory.

These were fateful times, but we, the British, had been given a God-given leader to hold our nation together, doggedly alone, resisting Hitler's master plan long enough for the giant American industry to build up aircraft production, ship building and

43

armaments to add to our own and the Commonwealth's so that together we could overhaul the vast Nazi war machine.

In the meantime, Winston Churchill had kept the American president, Franklin D Roosevelt, fully informed in detail about our plight. He was convinced we could withstand the Nazi onslaught, providing we replaced the much needed armaments lost at Dunkirk. Many people abroad did not think that we could resist Nazi Germany alone and that Britain could go under at any time. Fortunately, Roosevelt had faith in Churchill and believed his words. The result was that the Americans cut deeply into their reserve stocks of armaments, mainly manufactured in the war of 1914–18, and immediately despatched a huge supply which was ready for shipment by 11 June.

All through July this great tonnage of weapons and ammunition was ferried safely across the Atlantic, which filled a gaping hole in our arsenal and gave us the power to resist, and gave our forces the confidence to carry on alone against a strong and ruthless enemy.

Winston Churchill had carefully studied the subject of a possible German invasion of the British Isles with his top military advisers, and seriously believed that we could resist them because the Germans, at that time, did not have the right craft to land large numbers of troops and mechanised transport along our variable coastline. Thankfully the English Channel was our salvation.

10 June – Yet another overlapping situation has arisen. A blow is struck by Mussolini as he senses that Hitler is on a winning streak and decides to join what he feels would be the winning side. He, therefore, with Hitler's approval pushes Italy into declaring war on the UK and France. This, however, is not so popular with many Italians as Britain had long been a friendly nation towards Italy. It became essential that we declare war on Italy.

14 June – Paris falls to the Nazi horde. Paris weeps.

15 June – The Russian Bear awakes and in due course pulls in Lithuania, Latvia and Estonia. This makes Hitler wince with annoyance, but he can do nothing about it at this time because of his pact which is still in force with the Soviets.

By 16 June many meetings and discussions between Britain and France had taken place about how to continue the war against an overpowering enemy. There had been a plan for a Franco–British Union, with M Reynaud, the French Premier at that time, to take most of his Cabinet to Africa. Mr Churchill and the British War Cabinet wanted to give M Reynaud as much support as possible and issued a draft declaration. It was clear that we would only move towards an agreement if the French fleet was sailed to British harbours pending negotiations. There was also concern about the possibility of a French armistice. The defeatist section of the French government led by Marshal Pétain, then confused and cobbled any movement towards a Franco-British Union.

The French Army was by now in the final stages of withdrawal on all fronts. General De Gaulle and M Monnet and others flew to the UK to talk to Churchill about the gravity of the situation. A plan was laid and they return to France. In France Marshal Pétain and General Weygand decided to ask for an armistice because so much French blood had been shed. Unfortunately, General Weygand, a highly religious Roman Catholic, believed that France was being punished by God because she had stopped being a truly Christian country. He also foolishly believed he could make an honourable armistice with Hitler and hold France together.

General de Gaulle had quietly agreed with Winston Churchill that the only way to fight the Nazis was from across the Channel in Britain, and it was right that we should hold back the main part of our fighter squadrons in Britain rather than squander their entire strength in a losing battle in France, as Pétain and Weygand had initially requested. It was better strategically to do this and keep Britain alive for the future. Only at a later stage would France have the chance of living again, rather than remaining under the boot of the Nazi horde.

17 June – A well-planned flight to Britain by General de Gaulle, who was keen to carry on the fight against the invader, took place in the twinkling of an eye, as he stood on the tarmac close to a small British passenger aircraft at the end of a joint Anglo-French meeting set up by Major General Spears.

18 June – At this point the French Government was situated in Bordeaux. Discussions had already taken place about moving part of the government to form a centre of power in North Africa, away from the influence of the Nazis. Initially, Pétain was not averse to this idea, and President Lebrun would have readily agreed. There was much confused thinking. Then rumours about this proposed exodus reached the ears of General Weygand, who flipped. He believed this would wreck the honourable armistice agreement which he thought he could get with the Germans, which in fact had already begun round the back door via Madrid on 17 June. Laval was also alarmed as he was banking on a top job for himself in the proposed new French government under the Germans, and set up a unit to resist the 'exodus team'.

In the meantime Admiral Darlan, fervently loyal and the darling of the French Navy, who appeared to hate the British as much as the Germans because his grandfather had been killed at the battle of Trafalgar, had now become the new Minister of Marine. He thought it a good idea to pack off the leaders of the 'exodus team' and his critics to North Africa. He arranged, with the consent of the new Cabinet, to dispatch this enthusiastic freedom group on the *Massilia*, an auxiliary armed cruiser, to Casablanca. During the voyage, on 23 June, the ship received a radio message that the Pétain government had accepted and signed an armistice agreement with Germany. The three key members of the exodus group on board were Mandel, Campinchi and Daladier. Directly they heard this news, Campinchi tried to get the ship to change course to England, but the captain had probably been forewarned and refused.

When the ship docked in Casablanca, Mandel, together with Deladier, tried to start a resistance group, and Mandel contacted the British Consul. They set up their administration in the hotel Excelsior and made an announcement through a news agency. Unfortunately, a certain General Noguès picked up the message and reported this to the new French government, now moving to Vichy under German influence. They at once changed their minds about keeping a freedom section in North Africa, no doubt because of the armistice.

Mandel was arrested at his hotel, but the local French

magistrate in due course declared there was no case against him. Again Governor-General Noguès stepped in and re-arrested Mandel in the name of the new Vichy government and dismissed the magistrate who had released him. Mandel was then held on board the *Massilia*, which was in the harbour. Contact with the shore was forbidden.

News got to the British that a number of Free French were also held on board, but no plan could be devised to release them. This story ended later when Mandel and his comrades were brought back to France and treated as escaped prisoners. Eventually, years later, Mandel was murdered on German orders in 1944.

The French Navy was the source of much discussion between the British and French before the Pétain armistice was finally agreed by the Germans. Many situations had been aired. If Hitler had gained control of the large French Fleet it would have severely jeopardised our command of the sea war which was so vital to our survival.

General Weygand did not want the French Fleet moved away from French ports as he again pronounced it would finally frustrate his honourable armistice with Germany. Marshal Pétain would eventually fall in behind this assumption as he was getting anxious about the new government.

Admiral Francois Darlan had already said to Churchill that he would make sure that French ships would never fall into German hands. However, he would have to play his cards close to his chest when the Germans were in control. Churchill noted this remark with hope, but saw not a single French ship move to a safer haven away from the clutches of German control.

'Catapult' was the code name for a masterly British stroke to take over or disable a large part of the French Fleet remaining afloat in various locations. A number of French ships in British ports were taken over by the Royal Navy and carried on the sea war with their French crews. Some resisted, as they believed they must take their orders from the new Vichy government, and in one case a short sharp fight against the boarding party resulted in two deaths and three wounded.

Churchill and his advisers decided that Britain could not risk any French ships falling into the hands of the enemy. The 'Catapult' operation was timed for 3 July 1940 to be struck at daybreak. This action was vitally important for Britain, standing completely alone at this time, and was to take the French naval commanders by complete surprise wherever they were.

Admiral Somerville had one of the most painful tasks to perform in the name of His Majesty's Government. His duty was to offer Admiral Gensoul of the French Fleet in the Western Mediterranean the opportunity to bring his ships away from Vichy influence and join the British on the most generous terms in a united front against the Axis powers. Another option was to bring the ships, under Royal Navy control and with reduced French crews, to a British port, the reduced crews to be repatriated in the shortest time. Alternatively, if the French admiral felt that his ships should not be used against the Germans or Italians unless they broke the armistice, then the ships could sail with the Royal Navy, with reduced French crews to a French port in the West Indies, or to the United States and then be disarmed.

If none of these offers were taken up, the British profoundly regretted that the French were to sink their ships within six hours, and finally if no action was taken the British Admiral had been ordered by His Majesty's Government to take whatever action was necessary to prevent the ships falling under the control of the Germans or Italians. The problem was that we could not take the slightest risk of the powerful French fleet falling into enemy hands. If the Axis succeeded in getting their way we could lose the war.

Initially the French admiral refused a meeting with a certain Captain Holland, who was sent by the British Admiral Somerville because he was known to be a good friend of the French. Next, the document laying down all the proposals for action was sent by messengers. To this Admiral Gensoul replied in writing stating that in no circumstances would the French Navy be allowed to fall into German or Italian hands intact and that force would be met with force. All day long negotiations continued. The British admiral was reluctant without a direct order from the Cabinet to open fire on his French naval comrades. It was an emotionally charged situation. Finally, the British War Cabinet issued a command that unless the French complied with the British terms before dark and sank their ships, the British Navy would do it for them.

At 5.54 p.m. Admiral Somerville opened fire. By 6 p.m. his ships were heavily engaged with the French Fleet and the shore batteries of the North African ports which joined in. The bombardment lasted for some fourteen minutes and was followed by heavy attacks by naval aircraft from the *Ark Royal*. The attack was successful. One battleship was blown up, one ran aground, one was beached and one escaped but was damaged by torpedo aircraft.

The French Fleet at Alexandria, after considerable negotiations with Admiral Cunningham and the French Admiral Godfrey, agreed that all ships would discharge their oil fuel and remove vital parts of gun components, and also to repatriate some of the crews.

At Dakar some days later the French battleship *Richelieu* was hit by an air torpedo from our aircraft carrier *Hermes*, and seriously damaged. In the West Indies a French aircraft carrier and two light cruisers were immobilised after long negotiations with the United States.

By 4 July Churchill was able to report that the major part of the French Fleet had been disabled. It was all so sad, but oh, so necessary. Most of the powerful French Fleet had been removed from the clutches of the Germans and the Italians.

The new Vichy government now led by Marshal Pétain, called itself the Government of Unoccupied France. Upon receiving news about what had befallen the French Fleet on the North African coast, they decided to retaliate, and dropped a few bombs on the harbour of Gibraltar by aircraft from their African air stations.

On 5 July they formerly broke off relations with Great Britain. On 11 July President Lebrun gave way to Marshal Pétain, who was installed as Chief of State. This, however, did not really pull the wool over the eyes of the people, who in their agony understood what was happening to their country. Perhaps a glimmer of hope was just visible to them at this dreadful time.

49

A touching story emerged after the war about two French peasant families who both had sailor sons killed at the port of Oran on the North African coast during the 'Catapult' operation. At the funeral service which both families and their neighbours attended, it was requested that the Union Jack should lie side by side with the Tricolour over both coffins, and these wishes were reverently respected. Through the tragedy of the situation, a glimmer of hope seemed to have manifested itself.

Chapter Four
ALONE WE STAND

July 1940

As a nation we were now feeling the strains of war. Already, at my place of work, our ex-sales director who had been serving in the Navy commanding a torpedo boat had been reported killed in action. We were all in sombre mood. What would happen now? France was under the Nazi boot. Hitler by necessity would have to make the next move. He obviously thought we would give in after flattening all resistance so quickly with his large powerful mechanised army, but on the other hand the 'Catapult' operation must have shaken him somewhat.

As for myself and the people I knew, it was an amazing situation. We did not feel like a nation about to be invaded. We were in a war situation but the very last thought in my young mind was that we were doomed. Winston Churchill had done a wonderful job keeping up our spirits, but looking back on these times I can quite understand how many nations abroad thought that Britain was finished.

There was no doubt that Hitler and his generals were thinking and planning how best to invade our Island Home. This would be a different problem from rolling a large mechanised army across a land mass. The English Channel and the rest of the water around our coastline was in fact a very big problem for them. They must first neutralise both our very strong Navy and our Air Force. The Battle of Britain had begun.

From 10 July to well into August our convoys in the Channel were coming under heavier attacks, and gradually our ports from Dover to Plymouth were being systematically bombed. Hitler and his close advisers were already working on a plan named 'Sea Lion', designed to prepare a seaborne invasion of Britain. They were in the process of assembling self-propelled barges, tugs and small vessels, and they would also need to requisition more than half their major shipping transports. In the meantime the RAF was being expanded, but it was still quite small compared to the huge size of the Luftwaffe. Bomber Command was in the process of attacking anything along the French coast which appeared to be part of an invasion grouping. Coastal Command had a tough job on their hands helping to guard shipping in the Channel and watching for U-boats surfacing. Unfortunately the few aircraft they had were rather slow and were sometimes vulnerable to Me. 109's. British fighter squadrons also swept the Channel in an effort to protect shipping and report on U-boat activity.

Following the evacuation from France, the British Army was being further trained and equipped and in greater numbers in the homeland than ever before. Additionally, the home guard, made up from localised groups of men, all volunteers and of all ages not in the regular Army, were ready and trained to help fill gaps in the defences. Weapons, however, were somewhat restricted due to our rapid retreat from Dunkirk to save men rather than hardware. Much equipment had to be abandoned at short notice.

Our everyday lives as civilians carried on as before. Food was of course rationed, but there were special restaurants appearing where one could buy a simple plain meal at a reasonable price. I went to the office every morning by District Line train, arriving at Cannon Street Station in the heart of London. At this time in the UK, as civilians we had not really experienced the wrath of Adolf Hitler and his Nazi gang on the ground. Most of the activity was in the air and at sea. A few areas such as coastal ports had been bombed and airfields had received some attention, but unless one lived in these target areas it was something one heard about on the radio or read in newspapers.

Winston Churchill had the knack of teasing Hitler in his radio broadcasts, suggesting that any attempt at invasion would result in a severe thrashing of German forces. The British Bulldog spirit was given a good airing.

Then came the next phase. It became obvious to the German High Command that they could not proceed very far with their 'Sea Lion' plan until they had knocked out the RAF fighter squadrons.

And so it was that Reichsmarschall Goering was wheeled on to centre stage to clear the air of British fighter aircraft. The Germans needed to control the air over the Channel and initially flatten our airfields. Goering believed that the much larger numbers of German fighters and bombers would eventually swamp our defences, but the German naval commanders responsible for sailing the German invasion forces across the Channel were not quite so confident.

The two British fighter aircraft, namely the Hawker Hurricane and the Vickers-Armstrong/Supermarine Spitfire shouldered most of the daylight interceptions of German aircraft. The Hurricane was very manoeuvrable and the Spitfire was somewhat faster and very useful at a higher altitude. Both aircraft were heavily armed, initially with machine guns, depending upon the requirement. All guns were positioned in the wings and all fired outside the arc of the airscrew, arranged to give maximum effect at a given distance. At this stage our squadrons had far more Hurricanes in service than Spitfires. It was a delightful aircraft to fly, although the performance was not quite as sharp as the Spitfire which was designed at a later date. A few years later I was able to experience this for myself.

The opposition in the main was the Messerschmitt Me. 109, which escorted the German bombers. This was also a fast aircraft with a high rate of climb, but with a different configuration of armament. An important feature was one cannon firing directly through the airscrew hub and two machine guns synchronised to fire through the arc of the airscrew. It was not so heavily armed as the British fighters, but had the helpful feature of a direct line of fire.

For the civilian population at this time, it was a strange war. I can remember one sunny weekend in the open-air swimming pool in Barking Park, looking up into the sky and seeing a German aircraft calmly flying around, possibly on reconnaissance or lost, and then suddenly turning and changing direction, flying off without any of our fighters in pursuit.

Life suddenly became more of a hazard. At my place of work, a rota was worked out for the male staff to take turns at nightly fire-watching, as incendiary bombs had started to fall. The old dry roof structures of our office building in Bond Court, Walbrook were very vulnerable to firebombs, and it was vitally necessary for a close watch to be kept on the situation. Tin hats and stirrup pumps were the order of the day.

The war was now becoming as much a civilian problem as it was for the fighting services. I was surprised to find that my first partner in guarding the office roof against German firebombs was none other than our very important 'penny ha'penny adhesive stamp' company secretary. He became a different person under these strained conditions and almost affable, but as no air-raid siren had sounded he withdrew to his office to attend to some pressing business matter.

I had already enjoyed an upmarket wartime evening meal in the high-class restaurant in Walbrook at the company's expense. This in turn had given me, a seventeen-year-old office junior, a sense of well-being and a one-notch-up-the-ladder feeling of importance. The night wore on peaceably with no enemy bombers attacking London, and I even managed to get some sleep.

Heavy air fighting had continued through July and into August over Kent and the coast. Goering still believed the overwhelming size of the Luftwaffe would soon eliminate the effectiveness of our fighter strength, but he was wrong. Air Marshal Dowding had directed our fighter squadrons with great foresight, making allowances for our smaller overall number of available aircraft.

The massed formations of German aircraft were reported by the Observer Corps, which had grown into a large and important early alarm system. This, coupled with radar, which picked up formations coming in over the sea, and even from their airfields if close to the French coast, produced a very effective early warning for Fighter Command.

At 11 Group Operations Room, under Air Vice Marshal Park, this information was collated and plotted on a large table/map where WAAF and airmen staff would move markers continuously to show the position of our own fighters and the enemy formations entering Essex, Kent, Sussex and Hampshire. Our fighters could then be directed or scrambled to meet the enemy head on, thus saving fuel and taking the enemy by surprise.

Losses of aircraft on both sides were high, and according to our figures the German losses were much higher, but accuracy was difficult as sometimes more than one pilot claimed the victory of an individual aircraft after some intense activity, which was understandable in the heat of action.

Our own fighter pilots at this time have been honoured in history as the 'First of the few'. They did a tremendous job, sometimes tired out and utterly exhausted from continuously taking on large formations of enemy aircraft. They physically held back Hitler's plan of invasion. Eventually there came the point where the RAF was becoming short of experienced pilots. Our new young pilots sometimes became vulnerable to the greater number of the enemy, who often had more flying hours' experience from their fighting in Poland, Norway, Holland, Belgium, France and more recently in the war at hand. However, the Luftwaffe found that large as it was, it had not been able to clear the air of British fighter aircraft.

By 15 August much air fighting had been going on, and bombing of our southern ports. Goering and his close team of planners decided on a two-pronged air attack which they thought would break the back of the RAF fighter squadrons. They sent in excess of 800 aircraft to the South of England to bomb airfields where most of our aircraft were concentrated. In addition they sent a force of about a hundred aircraft to flatten Tyneside, made up mostly of Heinkel 111 bombers, escorted by Me. 110 twin-engined long-range fighters – the latter necessary for the range, but with inferior performance.

Air Marshal Dowding had fortuitously laid off seven fighter squadrons from the South of England for a rest and to cover the North. When the above German force flew in towards Tyneside, believing most of our fighter squadrons were down in the South, they were surprised yet again to meet a formidable array of British fighters, who shot down thirty German aircraft, mainly bombers, with the loss of only two aircraft with the pilots injured. This was the last time the Germans tried to bomb us in daylight without the protection of their shorter range but efficient Me. 109 fighters. This meant that any target north of the Wash was free from attack by day.

The 15 August became the date of the largest air battle of the war so far, with a combined total of losses calculated from reports at the time, covering all the actions in the North and South, of seventy-six German aircraft to thirty-four British.

At this time we needed more new aircraft and replacements quickly. It seemed an impossible task to accomplish, but Lord Beaverbrook stepped into the breach, cut through the red tape and produced a flow of spares, repaired aircraft and new aircraft. These were delivered to the squadrons, vastly improving the overall situation. Winston Churchill was so pleased with this performance that Lord Beaverbrook was invited into the War Cabinet. In addition Ernest Bevin, Minister of Labour and National Service, welded the nation's workers together to give maximum production of munitions in a surge of selfless patriotism. He too joined the War Cabinet in September.

Large numbers of German aircraft continued to bomb our airfields, and we lost a number of heavy bombers on the ground. The raids became more numerous, with bombs falling over wider areas. Large formations of German aircraft were creating a toll on our smaller number of fighters, and even though our squadrons were tearing into the enemy, it has to be said that if Goering had stayed with his initial plan of hammering our airfields and fighter strength it would have completely saturated our resistance, but at this point he made a tactical blunder.

Towards the end of August, in reply to sporadic German air raids on London, the RAF retaliated and bombed Berlin. This was a fairly small affair because of the distance our aircraft had to travel, but it surprised and infuriated Hitler. Never let it be said that we bombed Berlin before they bombed London or any other city. When the Germans bombed London they had the advantage of using airfields along the French coast, which made London a much closer target.

The date for the German 'Sea Lion' invasion had been put back because they simply did not have command of the air over the Channel or over Southern England. The German Navy could not possibly launch and shepherd an invasion whilst the RAF was so active. Hitler wanted results and Goering was in the hot seat. All eyes were on him to improve the situation. His plan was to drop more and more bombs on towns in the South East and his aircraft started to make heavier night attacks upon London.

At first we tried using night fighters, Blenheims and Defiants, with no outstanding success. Then the Army tried using anti-aircraft fire, but apart from making a lot of noise and impressing we civilians, they in turn had little success. Gradually, however, techniques improved for both night fighters and anti-aircraft gunners, alternating at different times and gaining better results.

My parents and I were still living in our small house in Barking, and every night we listened for the air-raid alarm. Sometimes in our area the wailing of the siren would be heard, and when the guns started firing we knew the enemy was above and we would go into our Anderson shelter in the garden.

Shrapnel from the exploding anti-aircraft shells could sometimes be heard bouncing on roofs of houses and the road surfaces. My father would often be late arriving home because his bus had been diverted. It must have been a dangerous and harrowing time for him, never quite knowing where the bombs would fall, but he seemed to take it all in his stride.

Heavy explosions could often be heard in the distance, but we were really remarkably free from bomb damage in our immediate area at the time. This however, was not the case with areas closer to the London docks and the East End.

Goering felt that the nightly London raids would break the spirit of the British nation and we would eventually give in. This was his tactical blunder. The bombing brought great hardship and misery. Houses and whole streets were ruthlessly flattened in the London suburbs, against all the laws of humanity, but in a strange twist of fate the Germans had switched their massed formations away from bombing our airfields, which gave Fighter Command the breathing space it needed to re-equip.

Heavy night air raids on the London Docks created some serious problems, but the British spirit was at its best under adversity. Gradually these massed bombing raids reached the very centre of the City. Then one morning after a noisy night of air raids, I arrived at my usual place of work after a considerably delayed journey, to find a gathering of colleagues standing in front of a heap of rubble where our office building in Bond Court had once stood. A German high explosive bomb had made a direct hit. Fortunately, the two colleagues who had been on fire-watch duty that night had been told to take cover in a subway as the raid had been so fierce, and they were unscathed.

Virtually the whole of the surrounding area was heavily damaged and more or less written off. However, the strong-room safe in the basement of 9 and 10 Bond Court, containing company records and the enormous metal-bound ledgers, were all intact.

A new office was very quickly organised and space was acquired in Bush House in Aldwych, along with another friendly company in the same trade. This was typical of the times we were all living through, and it is strange how everyone took situations such as this in their stride.

A single National Fire Service had been formed, amalgamating individual fire brigades, which did heroic service. Much has been written about their highly dangerous activities after these terrible air raids, where fire crews went into the burning rubble of collapsed buildings to save many lives, both young and old.

One wonders about the strategy of the Germans which followed. They appeared at times to be bombing indiscriminately without any plan. The air war continued in ferocity, with many German aircraft being shot down, but they still kept on coming.

In sixty-one days, from August to the end of September, Fighter Command lost 298 pilots and 615 aircraft. More pilots and aircrew were needed in greater numbers. We already had volunteers from the Commonwealth and the USA, and some ready-trained pilots from European countries which had been overrun by the Nazis. There were many Polish pilots, and some Czech pilots who had already been grafted on to our fighter squadrons and were hitting the Luftwaffe with a double vengeance.

From 7 September to 3 November approximately 200 German bombers attacked London every night. As days and weeks of bombing continued, the Luftwaffe found a new way of creating even greater devastation, by dropping land mines by parachute, sometimes fused to explode just above ground level. Yet another form of creating havoc and torment was the delayed-action bomb.

These produced a deadly game of finding ways to defuse these terrible weapons of destruction, referred to as UXBs (unexploded bombs). Sometimes these bombs were regularly fused bombs which should have exploded on impact, and had failed for some unknown fault. This situation was just as dangerous.

Special units called bomb disposal squads were trained and set up to deal with this problem, and some very brave soldiers lost their lives in this process. Many other towns and cities were attacked in a new wave of destruction, and on the night of 14 November, Coventry was heavily bombed. Approximately 500 German aircraft dropped 600 tons of high explosive and thousands of incendiary bombs. Four hundred people were killed and many more were seriously wounded. Coventry Cathedral was hit and became a ruin. Much of the time the Luftwaffe was targeting our industrial areas, but bombing at night was not yet an accurate science. A blanket approach did not bother the Nazis, even if it wiped out a cathedral and people in whole residential areas. Indeed they felt that bombing civilians would eventually make us surrender.

The following night it was London's turn again to take a battering, with more churches and monuments being hit. Then on three nights from 19 November, Birmingham became the target, with heavy damage and 800 people killed and 2,000 injured. Churchill visited the people of Birmingham a few days later and was amazed how the people had risen above their terrible ordeal to greet him.

And so the raids continued from the south to the north on ports and cities as far north as Glasgow. Then on Sunday, 29 December a huge concentrated incendiary bomb raid upon the City of London took place. Initially heavy high explosive parachute-mines preceded the firebombs, timed at the Thames low water hour, bursting water mains. This created problems for fire brigades. Something like 1,500 separate fires had to be fought. Railway stations and docks were seriously damaged and eight historic churches were virtually destroyed. The Guildhall was badly damaged, but St Paul's Cathedral miraculously survived the heavy night of bombing with a comparatively small amount of damage, mainly due to some energetic fire-watching against the incendiary cluster bombs. Surrounding buildings, however, in a great swathe nearby were completely gutted by fire and high-explosive devastation. The roughly curved layout of the original buildings on the south side of the cathedral were gone for all time.

King George VI and Queen Elizabeth had already experienced close bomb damage at Buckingham Palace and were pleased that they were able to share the dangers experienced by their subjects. Thus Hitler's wish to destroy the will of the British people had been reversed and made stronger. Eventually within the next few years German cities would get back what had been done to British cities with considerable interest. Such is war.

Whilst the battle was being fought in the sky above and bombs were raining down on our beloved country, much had been happening on the diplomatic front with our friends in the USA.

For many earlier months, the Royal Navy had been fighting a continuous sea war. The main object was to attack German surface raiders, aircraft and U-boats bent on sinking our merchant fleet, upon which our survival depended. British destroyers performed a vital duty protecting our convoys and were continuously at risk. A number of these had been sunk, and although we had a replacement ship-building programme in hand there was a dangerous gap growing in our fleet.

Churchill had held a long-running dialogue with President Roosevelt about this dangerous gap, and had suggested an arrangement to borrow fifty or sixty old American vessels in which we could quickly fit asdics against U-boat attacks, and in addition some flying boats. Roosevelt himself had listened to this request with great understanding, but there was a problem with the American Congress. They needed assurances that, should the Germans overrun the British Isles, our Fleet would carry on and defend our Empire, which of course included Canada, Newfoundland and the West Indies. Eventually it was broadly agreed, and Churchill told the Americans that we would never surrender or scuttle our Fleet and in fact that it was more likely the Germans would scuttle their own, remembering the *Graf Spee*.

The arrangement was described as friends helping each other

in time of need. At the time the Americans were anxious to protect their Atlantic seaboard, so we offered them areas on a 99-year lease which could be used to create naval and air bases. These areas were in Newfoundland, Bermuda, the Bahamas, Jamaica, Antigua, St Lucia, Trinidad and British Guyana. Both governments were in total agreement and all was finally settled. On 5 September, British crews were already standing by in America to bring back these fifty old vessels to be fitted out in the UK. Thus a vital temporary gap in our convoy escort duties would be filled. At this stage the USA was not yet officially at war.

With the fall of France and the Battle of Britain, this terrible war was indeed a World War, as other theatres were opening up and overlapping the whole time. It really was amazing how Britain managed to hold out alone for so long all through 1940 with all her European allies under the Nazi boot, and eventually standing firm against the combined effort of Nazi Germany and Fascist Italy.

With the Battle of Britain in full flow, Mussolini had been flexing his muscles. For some time he had his eyes on Egypt, and with the Germans throwing everything they could at Britain by air and by sea, one could read his thoughts.

When Mussolini declared war on us back in June it had been estimated that the Italians had 215,000 troops in North Africa. We however, only had approximately 50,000, made up of an armoured division, some British, Indian and New Zealand troops and two regiments of the Royal Artillery. Along the coastal road, which the Italians had built before the war from Tripoli to the Egyptian frontier, an ever-increasing number of Italian Army convoys streamed eastwards towards Egypt. The Italian Army had also gradually built supply depots and garrisons along the North African coast. With our mounting problems in Britain, Mussolini's dream of building a new Roman Empire must have started to become a reality in his greedy mind.

When Italy declared war, our small available British mechanised forces in Egypt immediately made some successful lightning attacks on forward Italian frontier posts. Prisoners were captured who had not even been told they were at war – a somewhat astounding state of incompetence.

Later, even after building a considerably well equipped army, they fared not much *better*. In the first three months after declaring war their casualties were almost 3,500 men, including 700 prisoners, against our losses of approximately 150 men.

The sea war in the Mediterranean had immediately flared. The old Italian cruiser the *San Giorgio*, was sunk by the RAF, and the Royal Navy had some considerable impact on the Italian Navy. Admiral Cunningham bombarded Bardia from the sea. Submarines were very active, and we destroyed ten of their vessels against the loss of three of ours from deep Italian mines. Then, whilst protecting a convoy on course from Malta to Alexandria, Admiral Cunningham took on a large powerful unit of the enemy, cleverly out-manoeuvring the Italian force, and the next day, at long range, hit an Italian battleship and two cruisers, without damage to the British ships.

The convoy was then attacked remorselessly by Italian aircraft over a further two days, but ultimately reached Alexandria safely without loss. The Italians never really lived this failure down and no doubt their allies the Germans were heavily critical. Ten days later an Australian cruiser, the *Sydney*, in company with British destroyers, sank another Italian cruiser.

The Mediterranean had now become an ongoing problem, with a large Italian fleet and air force to be kept at bay. We could not move large numbers of troops and supplies safely by sea for the North African campaign. The alternative was a long voyage down the west coast of Africa and around the Cape, which wasted precious time.

Ultimately, it is not possible for small numbers of isolated troops to hold back much larger armies on all fronts, so strategic choices have to be made. The Italians eventually entered British Somaliland on 3 August. This was not a particularly vital area in the scheme of things, so reluctantly, after losing the first position to overwhelming forces, and to avoid a total loss of life, the British General Godwin-Austen gave the order to withdraw on 15 August. Mussolini made great play of this, with much boasting and festivities, but his joy was short-lived.

Much thought was given to the passing of supply ships through the Mediterranean. Although the Italian Navy and Air

Force were quite large, their effectiveness was an unknown quantity. The naval engagements so far had shown that the Italian Navy, large as it was, had not been very successful, but they had some modern fighting ships which could become dangerous with more experience. Additionally, our British commanders were concerned that the Germans might suddenly decide to switch their main thrust to the North African campaign, which would make the Mediterranean passage an even greater hazard.

A serious effort was made to improve our fighter strength in Malta. As things stood three obsolescent biplane Gladiator fighters, known as 'Faith', 'Hope' and 'Charity', were the sole protectors of the island against aerial attack. In August twelve Hurricanes were successfully flown in from the aircraft carrier *Argus*. This was a much-needed boost to the fighter strength in the area.

It is not always appreciated how a fairly simple operation such as a fighter squadron move can suddenly become a deadly hazard. Fighter aircraft do not normally carry enough fuel for prolonged flights, and the endurance of the flight must be carefully calculated against the fuel carried.

In November, another fourteen Hurricanes took off from the same aircraft carrier, which was 400 miles to the west of the island. According to reports there was a change of wind direction. One could also visualise some heavy cloud building up. Tragically, nine of the aircraft, with pilots, were lost at sea as they ran out of fuel. Later, further flights took place successfully, with better margins of safety.

Aircraft in greater numbers were also required in the Middle East to combat the large Italian Air Force. The problem was delivering them safely and avoiding the perils of the Mediterranean. It was decided to ship the aircraft in crates to a suitable port on the west coast of Africa, assemble them and then fly them in hops across to Cairo. This took some considerable planning, as a journey of some 3,700 miles would need workshops and fully trained ground staff installed at every landing point en route. The West African port of Takoradi was selected as the starting point for this operation, and it was necessary for large workshops to be erected before the first aircraft arrived.

Eventually all was made ready and the first shipment of a dozen crated Hurricanes and Blenheims arrived in Takoradi on 5 September. This was followed by an impressive arrival of thirty Hurricanes flown in from the carrier *Argus*. In due course all these aircraft were gradually serviced and flown across the African continent in hops, taking four days to reach Khartoum, then on to Cairo.

However, quite soon the climate at Takoradi and the malaria produced some problems for the maintenance staff, which slowed output. Additionally, some aircraft developed engine problems en route due to the dust and sand encountered and were held back at landing points awaiting spares. Bad weather also created delays and overall it took time to improve. By the end of the year only 107 aircraft had arrived in Egypt via this air route. Further deliveries of aircraft into Takoradi by carrier were somewhat limited due to naval requirements in other directions. At least some aircraft had arrived in Egypt and made ready.

Yet another overlapping campaign started on 10 September. It transpired that part of the remnant of the great French Navy now under the Vichy government, comprising three cruisers and three destroyers, suddenly slipped out of Toulon. This coincided with a secret plan for General de Gaulle and Free French forces with British help to land in Dakar, a significant French colonial port on the west coast of Africa.

The idea was to make a bloodless occupation. However, this became complicated as a vital intelligence message on 9 September indicating that Vichy naval vessels were preparing to leave port was not acted upon. Additionally, a second alert via our naval attaché in Madrid on 10 September, also did not reach the First Sea Lord. It was only when the British destroyer *Hotspur* sighted the Vichy naval squadron at 5.15 a.m. fifty miles to the east of Gibraltar on 11 September, that the message reached him and things started to happen, but alas too late. The British line of communication had broken down for various reasons.

The Vichy naval squadron had slipped through the net and reached Dakar with sufficient forces to create a situation whereby the peaceful arrival of General de Gaulle was in jeopardy. Some high-level British naval officers had egg on their face after this fiasco, but there was so much going on at the time that the matter rested there, with a few rumblings.

It would appear that the Vichy government had been tipped off by a sleeper in the UK, although our own intelligence knew what the Vichy French were up to. The messages had been filed into the wrong tray! Extensive plans involving many men, ships and equipment had been involved.

Then on 19 September Admiral Pound reported that some Vichy French cruisers were leaving Dakar on a southerly course. The next day the Vichy cruisers were located at different times by the Royal Navy. The *Primauguet* was intercepted by HMS *Cornwall* and HMS *Delhi* and escorted back on a northerly course into Casablanca. The Vichy cruisers *Georges Leygues*, *Montcalm* and *Gloire* were shadowed by HMS *Australia* and later joined by the *Cumberland*. The cruising speed was suddenly increased, but shortly the *Gloire* lost power and was overhauled by the British ships. Her captain also agreed to return to Casablanca. The remaining two Vichy ships were lost in a rainstorm and managed to slip back into Dakar.

By 23 September both General de Gaulle and the British Major General Irwin were bitterly disappointed about the failure of the bloodless arrival. They wished that an attempt to regain the initiative should be made immediately. Officially we were not at war with Vichy France. De Gaulle then sent in two aircraft which landed at Dakar airfield. The pilots were immediately arrested by Vichy officials. One pilot held a list of Free French supporters. The two Free French emissaries sent under the tricolour and a white flag were snubbed. Following this incident further Free French supporters entered the port in launches and were fired upon. Two members were wounded.

The British fleet moved in through a sea mist to within 5,000 yards. The Vichy harbour battery then opened fire on a British destroyer. Fire was returned, and the engagement commenced.

The Vichy shore batteries along the coast, now manned by crack navy and army gunners landed earlier from the Vichy cruisers, were accurate and efficient. They also had gun-power on their berthed cruisers. The battleship *Richelieu*, although not in a seaworthy condition, could still fire double salvos from her 15-inch guns.

Sea fog prevailed for much of the day. Two of our destroyers were slightly damaged, and the *Cumberland* was hit in the engine room and had to withdraw. One Vichy submarine was bombed at periscope depth by an aircraft, and one Vichy destroyer was set on fire. Heavy sea fog prevented further action.

In the afternoon a landing of General de Gaulle's Free French troops at Rufisque had to be abandoned, mainly because of dense fog. That night an ultimatum was sent to the Vichy Governor. To this his answer was that he would defend Dakar fortress to the last. Our commanders replied that they would continue the operation.

The following morning the shore batteries opened fire on our ships and *Barham* and *Resolution* closed and opened fire on the *Richelieu*. Later the *Devonshire* and *Australia* engaged a Vichy cruiser and destroyer. Both the *Richelieu* and the *Fort* were hit by 15-inch shells. The Vichy destroyer was damaged and the light cruiser set on fire. A Vichy submarine was forced to the surface by depth charges and the crew surrendered. The *Barham* was hit four times during this engagement but without serious damage.

The action was resumed on the 25th. The coastal batteries opened fire and the *Richelieu* started firing 15-inch double salvos. Visibility was much clearer but the commander of the Dakar fortress released a smokescreen which made it difficult for our gunners. Sometime after 9 a.m. our battleship the *Resolution* was hit by a torpedo fired by a Vichy submarine.

After this the British admiral decided to withdraw because of further danger from submarines in the vicinity. The *Resolution* was damaged but not lost.

When news of the situation reached the War Cabinet in London, it was decided that it was clear Dakar would be defended by Vichy to the last. There was little chance at this stage of this important port coming over to the Free French without some considerable effort. Vichy was still not officially at war with us. It was prudent to press no further as things stood.

In the meantime, General de Gaulle over the next two weeks became more successful and was accepted at Duala in the Cameroons. This became the stepping stone for the Free French advance in West Africa, so all was not lost. Churchill was impressed but wondered about de Gaulle's ambition. The Free French arrival in this part of Africa forestalled further Vichy incursion. Additionally, this aided the development of our air route from Takoradi to Khartoum, much needed for the delivery of aircraft for the Middle East campaign. We had also prevented some Vichy cruisers returning to Dakar. These would have been used to prevent the advance of the Free French in French Equatorial Africa.

The Vichy government still did not declare war on the British, but to show they were no pushover decided on 24 and 25 September to make air raids on the docks and harbour in Gibraltar. In the second raid they used something like a hundred aircraft, but as Churchill commented the pilots did not seem to have their hearts in the attack. Some damage was done but there were not many casualties. Many bombs dropped harmlessly in the water. The Gibraltar AA shot down three aircraft. There must have been many Frenchmen at this time ruled by the Vichy government wondering where their leaders were taking them. Of course, if Vichy moved against the Nazis, control would have been quickly taken from them.

In the last quarter of the year the war crept steadily outwards in all directions, with the Balkans gradually being sucked into the overall conflict. Mussolini was also threatening Greece, and wanted Italian troops to be allowed to enter the country for strategic purposes. Hitler was not too pleased about this as Mussolini had not kept him fully informed, but he decided to wait and see if the Italians were successful.

The Greeks refused, so Italian troops already in Albania moved across the Greek border at several points at the end of October. The Greeks, however, were ready for the Italian push and resisted strongly. They also asked the British government for assistance under the assurances previously given by Mr Chamberlain. King George sent a message of confirmation to the King of the Hellenes, saying in so many words that their cause was our cause and we would fight the common foe together etc.

In the Mediterranean the Royal Navy had so far been successful against the Italian fleet (which was much larger in this theatre), and was taking steps to strengthen the situation. On 30

September it was agreed that the aircraft carrier *Furious* should return to the UK quickly to bring back more aircraft and pilots. The Italians at the time also had many more aircraft than we had in this area and a number of submarines which combined could be a serious hazard to our shipping.

Much thought was being given to protecting Crete and giving assistance to the Greek defences against the Italians. Already an RAF Blenheim squadron had been sent to Athens. More aircraft movements were being planned, but Winston Churchill could not understand why quicker relief for the Greeks was not taking place.

Anthony Eden, our Secretary of State for War, was in Cairo at the time. Official messages from Winston Churchill were pressing for more relief to assist the Greeks. However, in London the War Cabinet were not aware of the highly secret operation being planned by General Wavell and General Wilson. They had decided that rather than build up our defences against a massive onslaught from the Italians, which was inevitable, it would be better to take the initiative and use our smaller force of crack troops to attack them first. The operation planned was complicated. It was necessary to hit the Italians hard very quickly, in a number of fortified areas, with a smaller number of troops. Therefore there was a risk, but the plan was so good that the generals and their staff officers thought the risk worthwhile, but secrecy was essential.

It was too risky to describe this by telegram. Only when Anthony Eden returned home on 8 November could the details be given, by word of mouth. When Churchill and the War Cabinet heard the details of the plan which was to correct the balance of power in the desert, they were full of enthusiasm. They immediately understood why our generals were holding back our troops and equipment for the coming operation, which would require training and planning.

In the middle of these exciting events, the sad news of Mr Chamberlain's death on 9 November was announced. In spite of his preceding illness, up to a few days before his death he had followed closely every aspect of the war situation from the Cabinet papers which Mr Churchill had sent to him.

The operation, codenamed 'Compass', would involve some of our best fighting troops available in this theatre. The Italians had many more troops in fortified positions in the desert than we had, so the plan was complicated and involved a tight schedule and rapid movements. Much training had taken place, and indeed when the attack finally commenced, for security reasons the main part of the British force on a desert training exercise were suddenly told that in fact the exercise had now become reality and the assault on the enemy had actually begun. The thrust between Italian positions involved crack mechanised units of some 25,000 men of the Army of the Delta, travelling forty miles over the first night in the desert, laying flat down camouflaged by day and moving again by night without detection. It was a masterpiece of surprise.

On 9 December at dawn the battle of Sidi Barrani began. By nightfall several camps in the area had surrendered and many prisoners were taken. In the meantime the 7th Armoured Division had cut the coast road to the west and sealed off the area. At the same time on the 10th the Coldstream Guards, in their garrison at Mersa Matruth, opened up on the Italians in the position ahead at first light. The Royal Navy assisted with heavy fire from the sea. By 10 p.m. the Coldstream Guards had taken so many Italian prisoners they could not count them.

The rout of Italian troops continued on 11 December pursued by the 7th Armoured Division, the 16th British Infantry (Motorised) Brigade and the 6th Australian Division (which relieved the 4th Indian Division). By the 12th the whole of the coastal area around Buq Buq and Sidi Barrani were in the hands of British and Colonial troops. Prisoners were starting to pour into Mersa Matruth. The pursuit of Italian troops continued, with the RAF bombing and the Royal Navy shelling the coast road along which the Italian Army was retreating.

By 15 December all Italian troops had been driven from Egypt. This ended the first part of the battle around Sidi Barrani, which resulted in the defeat and destruction of the greater part of five Italian divisions. More than 38,000 prisoners were taken. Our casualties were small in comparison – 133 killed, 37 wounded and 8 missing.

General Wavell did not stop with his brilliant combined campaign. The 4th Indian Division, which had been relieved on 12 December was immediately moved to Eritrea to join the 5th Indian Division to fight the Italians in Abyssinia under General Platt. The journey took them by sea to Port Sudan, then by rail and boat up the Nile. All Indian Army units arrived between the end December and 21 January.

Mussolini by now must have become a very dejected leader. Only a few weeks previously, Admiral Cunningham had struck a blow at the Italian naval base at Taranto in the heel of Italy. Malta, being 320 miles from the target area, and with reinforcements of both Army and Navy recently installed, was the perfect springboard. High performance naval reconnaissance aircraft were now at hand and had brought back the necessary information.

The attack was made on 11 November. Two waves of aircraft flown from the aircraft carrier *Illustrious* were used to make a devastating raid on the well protected modern harbour. After dark, the first wave of twelve aircraft and the second wave of nine aircraft delivered the blow. Eleven carried torpedoes and the rest carried bombs or flares. The raid lasted an hour, with much activity. Three Italian battleships were torpedoed and one cruiser was also hit. The dockyard was also badly damaged. Apparently half the Italian naval battle fleet was disabled for at least six months. Only two of our aircraft were shot down by AA fire from a well fortified harbour.

By coincidence on the same day the Italian Air Force, by special request from Mussolini, carried out an air raid on the Medway in Britain, attempting to bomb our convoys. They used a bomber force escorted by approximately sixty fighters. They were intercepted by RAF fighters. Eight bombers and five fighters were shot down.

This was the first and last time the Italians attempted to raid Great Britain direct.

Chapter Five
THE CONFLICT WIDENS

As we entered the year 1941 I had now joined an Air Training Corps unit in readiness for my application for aircrew training in the RAF. Word had got around that this particular unit was a good one for getting results. The commanding officer, a headmaster of a school in East Ham, and his instructor staff all looked the part. He and one other wore RAF pilot's wings. The third member had a black patch over one eye, had no wings, and walked with a jerky limp which gave him a somewhat intrepid aura. They all dressed in RAF officers' uniforms, favouring the forage cap. I was suitably impressed. The cadets had to wear the official Air Training Corps blue serge uniform which buttoned uncomfortably up to the neck. After attending this unit every week, I gradually got the hang of things.

We studied all manner of useful subjects such as aircraft recognition, simple dead reckoning navigation, how to stand to attention and strut up and down a parade ground, and most importantly of all, how to present oneself at the crucial aircrew interview when one officially volunteered.

One day, when having a friendly chat with the least disciplined of the staff (in fact the somewhat knockabout character with pilot's wings), I learned that he had actually been a pilot in World War I. I was, however, somewhat disappointed to find that our commanding officer was able to sport a pair of pilot's wings for sitting in a basket under what I imagined to be a tethered balloon, used for observation purposes, also in World War I. Apparently, at the time ballooning qualified! To me this sounded more like something out of the Napoleonic Wars, but I understood it could be quite dangerous, when enemy aircraft took pot shots at the inflammable balloon and the occupants in the basket below.

The third member, with the black eye-patch and jerky limp, whom I imagined had either been in a nasty air crash or had been involved in some secret undercover operation, had in fact been suffering from an affliction since childhood. Sad, but quite out of character. And so my training proceeded. My office work in the City continued and my tasks continued to develop as male staff were gradually conscripted into the armed forces. However, my personal interest was really in other directions as I prepared for my own application to join the RAF.

One Saturday evening, after leaving a dance in Ilford Town Hall, (which was the general entertainment in those days for young lone males, either on leave or waiting to be called up), I was standing at a bus stop and started talking to a young sergeant pilot who had also been a pupil at a local school. I noticed with considerable interest that he wore his tunic with the top button undone, an unofficial sign that he was a fighter pilot. He was fairly short in stature and therefore fitted comfortably into a Hurricane or Spitfire. Interesting point – we all seemed to be shorter in those days. Some sixty years on the nation seems to be full of young giants!

The war dragged on in all theatres. It appeared that the Luftwaffe had been using radio beacons earlier in 1940, and then later in 1941, graduated to radio beams to find their way about, rather than the dead reckoning, map reading, radar and astro-navigation used by the RAF. The beams were an advanced technology.

Churchill referred to this as the wizard war, and no doubt the clever Germans thought they could find their targets at night in any weather conditions with more and more accuracy as their technology developed. We now know that our back room boys were clever enough to gradually crack the German beam systems, which became more and more sophisticated. Our boffins found ways of bending the German beams so that their aircraft sometimes bombed the wrong target, often in open country away from populated areas.

By 1941 we had the technology not only to bend the German beams, but also to fit out Blenheims, and later Beaufighters, with a special form of radar equipment which enabled the navigator/wireless operator to direct the pilot at night to a point within a hundred yards of the enemy aircraft before opening fire. A devastating advantage.

President Roosevelt was doing his utmost to make Congress appreciate our position regarding payment for the vast quantity of goods and armaments required to fight off the Nazi menace. Already an American warship had collected from Cape Town all the gold we had accumulated at that point. This, and the favourable appropriation of Courtaulds by the USA, were the rather unpopular actions which took place. Things eventually smoothed the way for the Lend-Lease agreement in March 1941, which enabled Britain to get all the supplies needed to fight the war and stay free. In Roosevelt's own words, 'America must be the great arsenal of Democracy'.

Looking back, it seemed that we had reached a situation where we were moving about inland more freely in the UK, without quite so many air raids. Possibly the Germans had lost so many aircraft in attacking our cities that they were conserving their aircraft for other activities in different theatres.

One of the most important features of the war at this time was to keep open our vital supply line across the Atlantic Ocean. The Germans were now making a concentrated effort using every kind of activity to break our lifeline. The U-boats were already taking a heavy toll on our shipping, and more and new longer-ranged U-boats were coming into service. Additionally, German Fokke-Wulf aircraft of long-range capability were prowling the ocean and directing surface raiders and U-boats towards our convoys.

They had failed to bring us to our knees by bombing our homeland, so now they would concentrate on depriving us of much-needed food, ammunition and armaments by sinking our merchant fleet. However, despite these horrors, more and more vessels were being fitted with asdics, and we were stretching our escort vessels to the full. The Americans, although still not officially at war, were giving us help by allowing our damaged warships and merchant ships to be repaired in American shipyards. They also supplied some aircraft which included Catalina flying boats, ideally suited for hunting and reporting U-boat activity in the broad ocean.

The Royal Canadian Navy stepped up production of corvettes in Canadian shipyards, and was then able to give escort protection of convoys in the western part of the Atlantic. The Royal Navy would give protection in the eastern part of the ocean. Consequently, convoys had full and intensive cover over the whole voyage, which helped considerably.

As the year progressed, the German advance through the Balkans developed. Early in April the German army invaded Yugoslavia and Greece. Once again the Luftwaffe quickly bombed all resistance and they pushed everything before them. An intensive air attack on the Greek port of Piraeus caught British merchant ships unloading cargo, and one ship with 200 tons of TNT on board was hit, virtually wiping out the whole port. Same old story; there were insufficient British aircraft around to fight off the weight of the Luftwaffe and stem the German advance.

In North Africa by the end of March the German forces were gradually moving into various strategic areas where the Italians had lost ground. Already German armoured units and aircraft had started to strengthen some Italian forces in Tripolitania, which would become a threat to the British and colonial forces in Egypt and Cyrenaica. Hostilities would inevitably run to and fro, across the desert with many situations arising both good and bad until we acquired our full strength with aircraft, tanks and armour in all its forms to support our infantry. General Rommel was now in command of the Afrika Korps. The enemy again had close support from the Luftwaffe, and German troops and armour were beginning to back up the Italians.

Under pressure our forces were falling back on the night of 6 April, and an orderly retreat was in progress. Field Marshal Wavell had gone to the front to put General O'Connor in command, but because he was unwell it was decided that General Neame would continue with the command, and General O'Connor would impart his expert knowledge of the area to General Neame as things progressed.

At this point, because of the heavy traffic on the coastal road due to the 9th Australian Division's retreat from Benghazi, the two generals decided to take a quieter route on a secondary road without an escort, and were suddenly stopped in the darkness of the night. Behold, the guns poking through the windows of their vehicle were being held by a patrol of German soldiers. They were taken prisoner and their war had come to an abrupt end. This created a problem for Wavell which was unexpected and required the immediate revision of his forward planning.

It became necessary to stop or limit the use of the port of Tripoli for the entry of German and Italian reinforcements. Bombing attacks by aircraft had not produced the desired effect. Ultimately, after much consideration, it was decided that the only way to really break up the base and port facilities was by naval bombardment, but the risk to valuable naval vessels was high. Eventually, a surprise attack by the battleships *Warspite*, *Barham* and *Valiant*, and the cruiser *Gloucester*, plus destroyers, carried out a devastating bombardment on 21 April from a range between 11,000 and 14,000 yards during daylight hours for forty minutes. They then withdrew without any damage to our ships, to everyone's amazement. Much damage to the port was achieved. Enemy shipping in the harbour also sustained considerable damage and fuel depots and buildings were set on fire. Mission completed.

By the end of April we had to evacuate our army from Greece. The success of the withdrawal, to save over 50,000 men, was down to Admiral Cunningham and his highly efficient naval commanders. As the conflict continued to expand and develop in all theatres, the fortunes of war fluctuated day by day. Great Britain and the British Empire, as it was at the time, still stood alone against the tyranny of the combined strength of the German Nazi and Italian Fascist regimes, with some added complications from the Vichy French government.

Crete was the next target for the sweeping German advance. It had been decided that our forces would do everything possible to defend the island for as long as possible because of its strategic position.

Reconnaissance aircraft alerted the Royal Navy to a German plan to invade by sea. Initially small craft loaded with German troops attempted landings around the coast, but most of these were wiped out by light British naval forces despatched to the area concerned.

Naval commanders risked much in holding back the German invasion where our larger ships were clearly visible in the fine clear Mediterranean weather. The enemy had a large air force equipped with dive-bombers and fighter-bombers which were very effective, particularly when AA ammunition was running low on some of our vessels. Unfortunately British aircraft were few and far between in this part of the Mediterranean at the time. Notwithstanding this, not a single landing of troops by sea was successfully made by the Germans over the whole period, and they suffered many casualties in the attempt. Therefore, they concentrated on an airborne attack on 20 May.

The German Air Corps was Hermann Goering's proud boast. It was built on the backs of the enthusiastic Hitler Youth Movement. Hitler himself was not so keen on the idea of a huge drop of parachutists, but Goering believed they would be invincible and pressed ahead with his operation. The Germans used large numbers of these highly trained and highly charged young Nazi parachute troops. Initially the airfields were heavily bombed. Then troop and equipment-carrying gliders landed close by, followed by large numbers of parachutists dropped from aircraft flying between 300 and 600 feet.

New Zealand and British soldiers with rifles were in perfect positions to pick off many of the parachutists before they even landed. German losses were extremely high. However, British heavy armaments were somewhat limited. This was followed by fierce hand-to-hand fighting, particularly in the New Zealand sector. Wave after wave of parachute troops were sent in by the German command, without heed to the loss of life.

The pattern of the German attack was the same on each successive day. Heavy bombing of the airfield and British and New Zealand positions. Then followed more troop-carrying aircraft, which landed or crash-landed wherever suitable. By the third day the Germans had gradually overwhelmed the Allied positions by sheer weight of numbers, but their losses to gain ground were high. Goering's prized airborne parachute division was virtually destroyed, losing around 5,000 men. Overall it was estimated that the operation had cost the Germans over 15,000 men killed and wounded, and had seriously weakened their forces in the area.

However, it was not without losses for our navy. To protect and evacuate our soldiers it was necessary to bring close to shore large naval vessels which became targets for enemy bombers, and dive bombers in clear weather. Three cruisers and six destroyers were lost. A further nine cruisers and destroyers went back to Egypt for repair. Additionally the battleships *Warspite* and *Barham* and the aircraft carrier *Formidable* were damaged and had to leave Alexandria for another port for specialised repair, along with some other vessels. Around 2,000 naval personnel were lost overall.

Towards the end of May, as the evacuation of our troops had started, the King of Greece and the British minister were taken off to safety, and on 30 May an attempt to evacuate the remainder of our troops was made. It was believed that a further 3,000 men still remained. In a risky operation on the morning of 31 May, two cruisers and three destroyers under the command of Admiral King filled their ships with our soldiers. Later they went back again at 3 a.m. on 1 June, making a final attempt, and brought out almost 4,000 men.

It then appeared that up to a further 5,000 British and colonial troops were still holed up in various parts of the island, and were given the order to surrender. However, a number of small groups and some Greek soldiers hid away in the mountains, and were helped by the villagers to survive. The Germans somehow found out that soldiers were still in hiding, and descended on the local people and ruthlessly shot them in groups of twenties and thirties in barbaric acts of reprisals.

Sixteen thousand five hundred British and colonial troops were brought safely back to Egypt by the navy. Our losses in the battle of Crete were reported to be around 13,000 troops who were lost, killed or taken prisoner.

It became painfully obvious that the vast numbers of German aircraft built up in the preceding years, before the aggressive Nazi drive for world dominance began, was the main key to their success. Until the balance was corrected these painful situations would repeat themselves, no matter how excellent in performance our smaller numbers of squadrons became.

Also in the latter part of May, it was reported that the new heavily armed and heavily armoured German battleship *Bismarck* and the new powerful cruiser *Prinz Eugen*, plus a strong escort, were preparing to enter the Atlantic. This could become another great threat to our shipping, in addition to the German battle cruisers *Scharnhorst* and *Gneisenau* and the cruiser *Hipper*, already holed up in Brest.

A strong force of the Royal Navy was immediately alerted and sent hotly in pursuit. At the time it was immensely serious, as we had eleven convoys including troop ships which at some point could fall to the firepower of these highly efficient warships, quite apart from U-boat attacks.

Before nightfall on 23 May, the cruisers *Suffolk* and *Norfolk* (part of an attacking force to stop the breakout of this new danger) suddenly sighted the two German warships heading for the Denmark Strait between Iceland and Greenland, skirting the pack ice. The two British cruisers with great tenacity followed through driving rain and snow and kept the enemy in sight, reporting their position.

In the meantime the battleship *Prince of Wales*, the battle cruiser *Hood* and six destroyers were on a north-westerly course towards the action. Then in the very early morning of the 24th the *Suffolk* and *Norfolk* could see the *Bismarck* twelve miles to the south on a southerly course in the Arctic twilight. Soon the *Hood* and *Prince of Wales* came into view and it was clear that battle would commence.

The *Bismarck* was the very latest German battleship, with eight 15-inch guns; it was probably the heaviest armoured warship in the world at the time. With all this armour she still had a turn of speed to match the best. She was the pride of the German Navy.

The *Hood* opened fire at 25,000 yards with her 15-inch guns. The *Bismarck* replied and the *Hood* was hit, which started a fire in the 4-inch battery. All ships present were in action and the *Bismarck* was also hit, but the fire in the *Hood* spread alarmingly. She was not so heavily armoured as the German battleship, which had poured five salvos into the *Hood*. By now the whole of the midship was ablaze and suddenly she blew up. Tragically, more than 1,500 men, including Vice Admiral Holland and Captain Kerr, were lost. Only three of the crew survived.

The *Prince of Wales* had to avoid the considerable wreckage left from the *Hood* and then continued the action. Shortly she too suffered heavy damage and two of her 14-inch guns were out of action. It was prudent to withdraw, maintain contact and await stronger assistance which was on the way. However, she had actually damaged the *Bismarck* in the engagement and the German ship was leaking oil underwater.

Our faithful leader, Winston Churchill, with his tremendous knowledge, experience, and remarkable insight, would assess each situation as it arose. In this case, without knowing that the *Bismarck* was holed underwater, he was convinced that although we had suffered the tragic loss of an important warship, the captain of the German vessel had taken the wrong decision when he continued on a southerly course rather than return to a safe port after a conspicuous victory.

The two British cruisers and the *Prince of Wales* continued to follow the *Bismarck* and her escort throughout the 24th, although the *Prince of Wales* was badly damaged and her armament was somewhat depleted. Towards evening HMS *King George V* and her escort were converging on the enemy, but could not reach a point of action until 9 a.m. on the 25th. In a determined effort, British warships from all quarters were turning towards the action in an attempt to stop the *Bismarck* from breaking out. On paper it was a net thrown wide in the ocean, but the German battleship was a formidable problem; it seemed almost unsinkable. It appeared that our best ships were insufficiently armoured against these new German battleships. Royal Naval battleships *Rodney* and *Ramillies*, and the aircraft carrier *Victorious*, had all changed course towards the German pirate. At one point early on in the chase the *Bismark* had suddenly turned back and fired towards her weaker pursuers, but this was a blind to allow the *Prinz Eugen* to escape at high speed as she needed fuel, and would later refuel at sea before returning to port.

Admiral Tovey in the *King George V* was now commanding the overall attack. Nine Swordfish aircraft carrying torpedoes took off from the *Victorious*, protected by four cruisers. The aircraft had been sent ahead at 10 p.m. on the evening of the 24th to slow down the progress of the *Bismarck*. This was a flight of some 120 miles against a strong headwind in dirty weather with a low cloud base. They were guided to their target by HMS *Norfolk*'s wireless directions following the *Bismarck* at some distance. The Swordfish aircraft were somewhat outdated and slow, but highly effective if they delivered their deadly tin fish. The Germans knew this as they put up withering fire. It was really amazing how they managed to find the target in such conditions. Somehow all nine aircraft survived.

The return flight was extremely hazardous in such filthy weather, and to add to their problem the homing beacon on the *Victorious* had failed and so they were guided back to their roost by searchlights and signal lamps, risking an attack by U-boats. The Bismarck had been hit under the bridge but she sailed on at speed.

In the early morning of the 25th the *Suffolk*, zigzagging to avoid U-boat attack suddenly lost radar contact with the *Bismarck*, and it was thought that she had changed course for the North Sea. In the confusion that followed the *Bismarck* had slipped through the net and was now well ahead of the British ships in her run for safety.

The battleship HMS *Rodney*, a well armed vessel, was now moving towards the new course of the *Bismarck*, but alas she crossed ahead of the German vessel without making contact. The feeling began to emerge that the *Bismarck* had completely slipped the net and there was much disappointment.

Suddenly the situation changed again. From the south in the heavy Atlantic swell HMS *Renown*, the aircraft carrier *Ark Royal* and the cruiser *Sheffield*, under the command of Admiral Somerville, were believed to be on a converging course with the fleeing *Bismarck*. By 26 May in the early morning a number of the British ships were starting to run low on fuel and slowed down to conserve supplies. The exact position of the *Bismarck* was still not accurately known.

Catalina flying boats were called in from Lough Erne in N. Ireland, and one of these spotted the escaping German ship, which fired on and damaged the aircraft. All was not lost, as the Catalina had reported Bismarck's approximate position, some 700 miles from Brest, before returning to base. Within an hour two Swordfish aircraft from the *Ark Royal* spotted *Bismarck* again.

The *Renown* was now eastward of the *Bismarck* but needed heavier support before it became feasible to make an attack.

A certain Captain Vian in the destroyer *Cossack*, together with four other destroyers, had been ordered to leave their convoy duty to join in the hunt for the *Bismarck*. Having arrived in the area they were suddenly given the position of the German battleship from another patrolling Catalina. Without receiving specific orders, the five destroyers set course at speed for immediate action. The number of British ships accumulating in the area was starting to give some confusing views from the air.

Admiral Somerville, speeding northwards with his three ships, sent the cruiser *Sheffield* ahead to keep tabs on the *Bismarck*. The *Ark Royal* was not aware of this movement and launched a Swordfish air attack towards the *Bismarck*. With the number of ships converging in the area, the radar guidance system unfortunately led them to the *Sheffield*, which they attacked. Fortunately, due to some spontaneous evasive action by the British cruiser, they missed. The mistake was quickly rectified and the aircraft returned to the *Ark Royal*. The *Sheffield* eventually found the *Bismarck* and kept her in sight for the major attack to line up.

At around 7 p.m., fifteen Swordfish again became airborne from the *Ark Royal*, loaded with their deadly tin fish to find their target, which was now only forty miles away. This time they made good their previous error and pressed on with the attack, with guidance from the *Sheffield*. Within two and a half hours they had completed their operation and returned to their mother ship. They had made two positive hits on the *Bismarck* and possibly a third. Another aircraft involved in reconnaissance reported that the powerful German warship was seen to make two complete circles after the Swordfish attack and it appeared that she was out of control. Captain Vian's *Cossack* and accompanying destroyers at last arrived on the scene and throughout the night at every opportunity fired their torpedoes into the stricken *Bismarck* with her guns still firing.

Shortly before midnight, the German commander, Admiral Lutjens, signalled 'Ship unmanoeuvrable. We shall fight to the last shell. Long live the Führer'. Apparently German bomber aircraft then came out from the coast and U-boats arrived in an attempt to save the situation, largely to no avail.

The battleships *King George V* and *Rodney* arrived within the area by the morning of the 27th and found that the *Bismarck*'s armament was still mainly intact, and therefore dangerous, but she was steaming in the wrong direction. First the *Rodney* opened fire, followed by the *King George V*. The *Bismarck* returned fire and straddled the *Rodney*. Very soon the British ships got the upper hand and the *Bismarck* stopped firing. By now she had a fire amidships and a heavy list to port. By 10.15 a.m. her mast had been shot away and she was silent. She was a smoking hulk, but still did not go down. It took several more torpedoes to finish the job and she finally sank. There was no doubt this had been the strongest battleship in the world to date and could have done tremendous damage to our convoys if she had survived. It was torpedoes fired from the British cruiser *Dorsetshire* which delivered the *coup de grace*. Admiral Lutjens and almost 2,000 of his crew were lost. Just 110 survivors were rescued by the Royal Navy. The rescue operation however, was cut short as a U-boat arrived on the scene and the British ships had to withdraw. Five more German sailors were rescued later by another U-boat and another vessel.

And now the great blunder that Adolf Hitler was about to make was his overall plan to defeat the Soviets. Hitler had forged an alliance with Stalin to hold things together whilst his cunning scheme was prepared. The Russians had failed to read the situation.

The German forces on the whole had been very strong, with considerable reserves of aircraft, armour, arms, ammunition, equipment and specialised shipbuilding. This plus a huge army had been prepared well in advance of Hitler's bid for world domination. The speed of his initial successes had been phenomenal and cruel. It would take something like two to three years to build anything like a full-scale resistance to stop his march. All we could do in the meantime, with the forces of Britain and the British Empire standing alone, was to slow him down and hold him back as far as possible at every point of incursion.

This we did quite successfully, despite some setbacks and

losses. With the foresight and experience of our great leader Winston Churchill, Hitler's dream was taking somewhat longer to materialise than he had hoped. Five or six weeks' delay in an overall campaign can produce some quite devastating changes to a master plan. And this became the crux of the Nazi miscalculation.

German forces had been tested and delayed in the Balkans and Greece, due to the presence of British forces. They also found it necessary to keep strong forces particularly in Yugoslavia due to a persistent uprising, which interfered with Hitler's ongoing battle plan to attack Russia. Eventually, after much military activity and movement of troops and aircraft, the Germans assembled large forces in Eastern Europe and also in northern parts of the Balkans. Finally the huge Nazi war machine was again ready to strike. At 4 a.m. on 22 June Ribbentrop delivered the formal German declaration of war to the Russian Ambassador in Berlin. In the early morning in Moscow, the German Ambassador, Schulenburg, did the same thing and presented himself to Molotov in the Kremlin. Molotov immediately commented on the fact that German aircraft had just bombed some ten unprotected Russian villages and could not understand why this had been done. The Luftwaffe then proceeded to flatten forward Russian airfields before any aircraft could get into the air.

The German excuse in so many words for breaking the treaty was, they said, because Russia had intensified attempts to undermine Germany in Europe. Secondly, Russia had adopted an increased anti-German foreign policy, and thirdly she had concentrated Soviet forces in readiness at the German border.

Our Foreign Secretary, Anthony Eden, had warned the Russian Ambassador in London several times of the Nazi movements, and the United States had given numerous specifically strong warnings to the Soviet Government, but Stalin chose to completely ignore all this advice.

Churchill was not at all enamoured with Stalin's regime, but he admired the Russian villagers for the way they tilled the soil in such a harsh environment, and how the men would fight for the survival of their families. When he was awakened on the morning of Sunday the 22nd the news of Hitler's invasion of Russia was brought to him. He immediately arranged to make a BBC broadcast that evening at 9 p.m. He set about preparing his speech with great care and thought and was only ready twenty minutes before the broadcast.

It is worth recalling part of Churchill's momentous words in this broadcast concerning this new and sudden turn of events:

> We have but one aim and one single, irrevocable purpose. We are resolved to destroy Hitler and every vestige of the Nazi regime. From this nothing will turn us – nothing. We will never parley, we will never negotiate with Hitler or any of his gang. We shall fight him by land, we shall fight him by sea, we shall fight him in the air, until, with God's help, we have rid the earth of his shadow and liberated its peoples from his yoke. Any man or state who fights on against Nazidom will have our aid. Any man or state who marches with Hitler is our foe... That is our policy and that is our declaration. It follows therefore that we shall give whatever help we can to Russia and the Russian people. We shall appeal to all our friends and allies in every part of the world to take the same course and pursue it, as we shall faithfully and steadfastly to the end.

He said much more in his BBC broadcast, but these words crystallised the situation at the time. Churchill also believed that Hitler did not trust Russia and wanted to make sure that they ceased to be any kind of a threat to his master plan. If he could bring Russia to her knees with his tremendously powerful army before the winter set in, he could then increase the size of an invasion force to invade Britain. This is what he wanted, to fulfil part of his dream.

The German invading force, with its mechanised armour again rolling across a huge land mass, did not find the Russian armies in a state of readiness to attack Germany, as stated in Hitler's declaration of war.

Hitler had already announced to his commanders that because the Russians were not signatories of the Hague Convention, the treatment of Russian 'prisoners' should not follow the Articles of the Convention. In other words they could be treated very badly. It appears that initially the German advance was rapid and ferocious, but gradually the Russian army awoke and slowed down the German advance.

Communications between Britain and Russia increased, as did messages between Churchill and Stalin. The war alliance between the two countries gradually moved into a higher gear. The Royal Navy became very active and sent some cruisers and destroyers to Spitzbergen to attack German shipping in cooperation with the Russian naval forces. Also some RN aircraft were being launched to attack German shipping off the northern coast of Norway and Finland.

It must be said that the Russians had kept mainly to themselves without getting involved in the war, right up to the time when Hitler suddenly turned their alliance on its head and invaded. Plainly Stalin had not expected this, but this inactivity had paid off in some respects, as large Russian forces were available up to this point, but not quite ready for Hitler's ruthless attack. The invasion front stretched across the complete frontier from the Baltic to the Black Sea. The longer the invasion lasted the stronger the Russians would become. They fought the Germans for every mile. The great land mass was eventually in favour of the Russian resistance. The heavily armoured German attacks were successful, but the overall advance was slow in proportion to the great distances which had to be covered. Russian casualties were large but their soldiers did not give ground easily. The Germans used something like 2,700 good aircraft supporting their armies, against the Russians 5,000 inferior aircraft, which suffered heavy casualties.

By the end of July it was obvious that Russia badly needed help with supplies of better aircraft. Churchill advised Stalin that arrangements would be made to assist, despite the fact that we needed every aircraft produced for our own struggle. This offer would take time to arrange, but by the beginning of September the equivalent of two squadrons of Hurricanes were shipped in HMS *Argus* to Murmansk to support and aid the defence of the naval base, and to cooperate generally with the Russians in the area. Additionally, 200 American Tomahawk fighters would follow as soon as possible – 140 would be sent direct from the UK, and sixty would be shipped from the United States. Spare parts and American technicians would follow to assemble the aircraft, and final arrangements were being made direct with the

American government. This was to show that we supported Russia in her bid to resist the Nazi onslaught. It was so important at the time as Russia was the one massive buffer which could soak up the strength of Nazi Germany.

The supply of aircraft offered would reduce our reserve supplies, but it was calculated to be strategically worthwhile. Of course, the number of better aircraft being sent to Russia did not address the balance needed, but it would give the Russian airmen more confidence, and show that help was on the way.

Several million pairs of ankle boots were also shipped, and raw materials of all kinds also followed as our own supplies built up with American help. The overall conflict involved very large numbers of troops on both sides. The Germans threw in something in the order of 164 divisions overall, which included armoured and motorised divisions. Twelve Finnish divisions and seventeen Rumanian divisions were included in the German total. The Russians assembled, as far as was known, 119 divisions to face the German advance, and also held sixty-seven additional divisions partly in Finland and partly in the Caucasus and Central Russia, making a total of 186 divisions overall.

The German armour and mechanised forces started to push forward with considerable success and were soon deep inside Russian territory. At the end of July there had been a disagreement between the German commander-in-chief, Brauchitsch, and Hitler. The former wanted to capture Moscow as the nerve centre, but Hitler wanted to take territory on a broad front and destroy as many Russian armies as possible. He wanted to overrun Leningrad in the north, and in the south to take the industry in the Donetz basin, the Crimea, and to take the Caucasian oil supplies.

Eventually Hitler won his argument and his commander-in-chief and generals reluctantly fell into line and moved around their forces in obedience to his wish. By the beginning of September the Germans had hemmed in a huge triangular pocket of Russian forces in the area Konotop–Kremenchug–Kiev, amounting to at least half a million men, who were either killed or captured in a month of bitter conflict. Hitler at this point must have strutted around with huge confidence in his own abilities.

Leningrad, however, was a different story. The Germans had surrounded the city but had not been able to take it. Hitler had made a miscalculation. At the end of September he then decided he must take Moscow. Large German mobile forces which had been attacking Leningrad were now again being shuffled back for another drive towards Moscow, including a detachment of aircraft. Their southern armies advanced eastwards where the Caucasus and the oil would be their target, which was only part of Hitler's plan.

Gradually we made arrangements to supply the Russians with many more front-line aircraft. As these started to arrive the resistance to the German advance stiffened.

A problem arose with the Polish government in exile. We, of course, had actually declared war when Germany invaded Poland. Later, Hitler had made an agreement with Russia to occupy certain bordering territories which had, historically, always been a sore point. Now that Germany had invaded Russia, and we had become Russia's ally, this arrangement could not be allowed to stand. The Poles would eventually require their lost territory to be returned.

This subject was very sensitive to Russia, but the overriding priority was the defeat of Nazi Germany. Therefore, it was decided that for the time being the subject would be put on hold, and that negotiations would have to take place later at an opportune time.

Churchill had close communications with President Roosevelt about the importance of helping the Russians increase their supplies of equipment. It was obvious this was now the best way to weaken the huge German fighting machine. Stalin kept pressurising Churchill to open up a second front in France, but this was an impossibility at the time, as the French coast had been efficiently fortified and an attack at that time would have been suicidal for Allied forces.

Eventually, after much planning with the United States, a conference in Moscow was finally arranged. Lord Beaverbrook would represent the UK, and Averell Harriman would represent the USA. Up to now, meetings with the Russians had been difficult. Their official attitude had been somewhat detached, surly, and at times unreasonable. Their armies, large in numbers but with inferior equipment, were fighting to the death. Something had to be done, and done quickly. Every week was important, and the Germans had to be stopped and held back until the harsh Russian winter set in, which could change the odds completely.

The Germans had made much progress, but they also found that battles were hard won. Russian partisans were attacking in the rear, and the Russian railway system, taken by the Germans, did not meet their requirements. The roads were breaking up under the heavy German vehicles and tanks, and the volume of supplies getting through to the front line was insufficient to meet their requirements.

It was clear from communications that the Russians needed many more good aircraft, armaments and tanks.

The Moscow conference was finally set for 28 September. The combined British/American mission arrived to a somewhat cold reception. However, once the intention to supply planned deliveries of aircraft, tanks and ammunition on a regular basis was spelled out, a thaw set in. From that point onwards the talks proceeded on a more friendly basis, and no doubt the vodka came out of the cupboard from time to time.

Britain was now cutting deeply into her aircraft, tank and armament requirement – from both the USA and her own production – to aid the Russian resistance. We still had to fight off the German air raids at home, and also to continue the fight in the Middle East and elsewhere. Our navy was continuously engaged on the high seas in all theatres, attacking the enemy and protecting our lifeline. Any reduction in our fighting ability through lack of supplies could be very serious. It was, therefore, a dangerous balancing act we were undertaking to aid the Russians.

The Americans were greatly increasing their overall production of aircraft, tanks and armaments to aid the fight worldwide against the Nazi menace. Russia would receive a large share of this production, but it would take some months for this to build up.

Already a plan had been put into motion, in cooperation with Russia, to improve the delivery route and upgrade the supply of front-line aircraft, armaments and materials to the Russian forces, through Persia (Iran). British and Russian forces had already entered Persia in unison on 25 August.

Field Marshall Wavell, based at the time in India, had planned the overall movement of British and Imperial forces for this short, sharp, but strategically important conflict. General Quinan, General Harvey and General Slim controlled the British campaign in the different areas.

There had been some considerable resistance by the Shah (who had good relations with the Germans) against the British troops making use of the Persian railway system. Eventually, after British troops captured the Abadan oil refinery, and moved to protect the oilfields and the employees of the Anglo-Persian Oil Company, the Shah announced a ceasefire. He then ordered the Persian troops back to their barracks.

British forces pressed on, but in the north they met more resistance. However, after the RAF helped things along, the Persian forces finally ceased fighting.

The railway system was gradually improved over many months and, with more locomotives and added rolling stock, produced an important bulk delivery link from the Persian Gulf to the Caspian Sea. This was particularly important for future shipments of American supplies for the Russian forces.

It was, of course, necessary to have the German influence in Tehran expunged and the German agencies completely shut down, which apparently took place. It was announced to the Shah that the British had no designs on his country other than the protection of the oilfields and the rail link to help the Russians fight the Nazis. Indirectly, the Persians would eventually benefit from an improved railway system. Much later the Americans helped with development of some additional road works to offer an even greater capacity for transportation.

This overall campaign created some unrest within the Persian Government which resulted in the Shah abdicating on 16 September in favour of his apparently gifted twenty-two-year-old son. On 20 September the new Shah restored the Constitutional Monarchy on the advice of the Allies.

At this time the campaign in the Western Desert was strangely quiet for some four and a half months on both sides, with General Auchinleck amassing his forces and equipment ready for an offensive in November. Rommel was also keeping his head down, as delays in various forms were hitting any plans for an immediate German offensive in the desert. Slowly the effect of the enormous battles raging on the Russian front, was starting to sap the strength of the Nazi resources.

Chapter Six
FORWARD AND BACKWARDS

As we moved into the autumn of 1941 many situations in this ongoing war were beginning to unfold. With the uncanny pause in the Western Desert, our strength, which was building up with better equipment, was also reflected back home in the United Kingdom. The supplies of better aircraft and armaments of all types were gradually trickling through to the Russian front from both the United States and ourselves. Of course, the sea and air hostilities continued and the Germans were still bombing our homeland, but with somewhat less frequency. On the other hand our own Bomber Command was increasingly giving back to the Germans some of their own medicine.

The Mediterranean Sea continued to be a dangerous place for shipping, with the Italian Navy still active with both surface warships and submarines to add to the German menace. It was, therefore, prudent in the main to send our large convoys around the Cape to reach our North African destinations with less risk. However, at times urgent heavily escorted shipments did venture through the Mediterranean, but with unavoidable danger.

Changes in the Australian government had created some problems with the deployment of Australian troops in Tobruk. These had fought courageously in the desert war and their government wished to pull them out for a rest. However, this created a difficult situation with Tobruk under siege. One infantry brigade had been replaced by a Polish brigade, and the navy had suffered casualties from enemy aircraft when bringing out some of the Australians. The overall plan was to prepare for the autumn offensive codenamed 'Crusader', and this would mean that no further replacements could be safely undertaken until November. However, even with further changes at this time within the Australian government, they still insisted on the relief of their remaining troops, despite the overall danger and problems being created. The situation culminated with HMS *Latona* being sunk and the destroyer *Hero* damaged by enemy air attack when attempting to collect the remainder of the Australian troops. There was a total of sixty casualties, including wounded and missing, on the *Latona*, but no Australians were on board. Admiral Cunningham declared that the remaining 1,200 Australian troops could not be moved until the dark nights in November.

Throughout November, at home in the UK, we were still making official preparations against a possible invasion by the Germans across the English Channel, which was the shortest route. We civilians did not think too heavily about this, but all the signs were there. The Home Guard would be used for specific duties if such a situation transpired, to back up the Army proper. Heavily reinforced pillboxes had already been built inland around the coast to give added defences amongst masses of barbed wire entanglements.

Of course, aerial reconnaissance was continuously in progress across the coast of France to establish if the Germans were assembling landing craft in large groups, but nothing very serious was reported. At the same time our Coastal Command, now equipped with some improved aircraft such as the twin-engined Hudson, was attacking anything which might hint at being in preparation for an invasion.

At last my own September application, via the Air Training Corps, for aircrew training upon reaching the age of eighteen, produced a response. On 19 November I was required to report to an RAF recruiting centre for attestation. The location turned out to be Oxford University, and I was required to stay for two days. The journey ended in the back of an RAF truck with a number of other 'keen types', and we were dumped unceremoniously, together with our two-day luggage in the back entrance of our destination. We all wished to become RAF pilots, but in reality we could also become either observers (as navigators were called at that time), wireless-operator air gunners or, if we were extremely unlucky, tail gunners, whose lifespan was known to be somewhat limited.

In due course the first hurdle to overcome was a fairly strict aircrew medical. I was a little concerned about my slightly flat feet. When it came to the foot test, I somehow willed my arches up a bit and went through the check piece – standing on toes etc. Apparently my feet were acceptable. I breathed a sigh of relief. Ears were important too. Whispering across the corner of the room with the outward ear plugged and the test ear towards the corner, was the standard required – no high-tech apparatus available in those days! Eyes were tested in the usual way by reading off charts, and night vision was also tested. Later I discovered that if one passed all tests and requirements and one's eyes were slightly below standard, flying goggles with special lenses were available.

We then moved to a college lecture room and were given a paper to answer which included some elementary trigonometry, being the basis of dead reckoning navigation. Finally, we were lined up for the all-important interview. There was no introduction or hint of who would assess each recruit. Suddenly I found myself being ushered into a room with an important senior RAF officer seated at a desk, whom as far as I can remember was an air commodore. I was pleased to note that he wore a pair of wings.

I had been advised by the Air Training Corps to wear my ATC uniform. Frankly, I always felt a bit silly in this uniform as it gave me the feeling of an imitation airman, and I seemed to be the only recruit in my squad wearing this outfit. However, following ATC guidance I snapped to attention and gave what I thought was a smart salute.

The interview proceeded, in what was to me a surprisingly friendly manner. I was not used to talking directly to the real flying fraternity, and it was a refreshing experience. I talked about my father being in the Royal Flying Corps in the First World War. I told the air commodore that I wanted to become a pilot and he indicated that I would receive a communication in due course regarding a decision. I saluted him and left the room.

I returned home with many thoughts filling my mind. The die was cast. Had I made the right decision? How long would it be before I became a serious contender in this ghastly war? Upon returning home my life continued much as before but in a state of limbo, still working in an office in the war-damaged City.

Vast amounts of territory and surrounding seas continued to be dogged by war. On the Russian fronts it appeared that Stalin and his generals were very secretive about their war plans. It was known that things were not going well and there was much bloodshed. The Germans were pressing hard on all fronts with their powerful armour and mechanised units, but not achieving the collapse of Leningrad and Moscow which they felt was vital to their campaign. By now any smaller country would have gone under, but as the Russian winter started to close in the great German war machine started to wobble.

Churchill wished for more open discussions with the Russians to devise an overall strategy, but the veil was kept tightly drawn. If the Russian armies could hold off the German onslaught for a few weeks longer the weather would really start to bite, and it did with a vengeance. As the German battle plan started to crumble, Adolf Hitler, in a fit of rage, removed his two top commanders, Brauchitsch and Rundstedt, and took command personally of his armies on the Eastern front, believing he could not fail and could produce a victory early in the spring of 1942.

In the Western Desert of North Africa, the 'Crusader' operation commenced on 18–19 November. The Eighth Army suddenly advanced in driving rain, taking the German Army by surprise. The fighting included tanks and armoured brigades, thrusting back and forth in surprise situations. Finally, by the first weeks of December 1941, after much fighting, General Auchinleck, with superb planning of his 'Crusader' operation, and even making a sudden change to his senior command on the spot, held the fortress garrison of Tobruk and broke the siege led by the German General Rommel. This was a great victory for the Eighth Army. Despite the heavier firepower of the German tanks, Rommel and his panzers were in full retreat. Another feature of this battle was the presence of the RAF, which gave close support to the British thrust in the desert. At last British aircraft were available in superior numbers to the Luftwaffe, and the effect was considerable – but no sooner had this victory taken place than a black cloud of misfortune swiftly followed.

In the meantime Hitler, with his thoughts sunk into Russian

battles and frustrations, suddenly realised that Rommel in the Western Desert had received a considerable setback. He immediately directed a transfer of a whole Air Corps from the Russian front to Sicily and North Africa. This in turn completely upset the balance of air power. Malta immediately came under heavy air attack and was struggling to survive. The Luftwaffe was again the master in the air covering the sea routes to Tripoli, which enabled a complete refit of Rommel's defeated armies. This would again, in due course, create more problems for our forces in the desert, as Rommel was an energetic and brilliant strategist.

On 7 December 1941 from another part of the world, the unbelievable news came through that the Japanese had suddenly attacked a major part of the American Pacific Fleet on a Sunday morning, peacefully at anchor in Pearl Harbor in the Hawaiian Islands. Fortunately the aircraft carriers and supporting cruisers were elsewhere at the time. Ninety-four ships of the United States Navy were in harbour, including eight battleships. Immediately, America had been dragged into the war. It became known eventually that virtually the whole of this mighty fleet had been wiped out with a cunning surprise torpedo, dive-bombing, strafing and kamikaze attack by 353 ship-borne single engine aircraft. The raid was craftily devised by the Japanese Admiral Yamamoto, without declaring war. More than 2,000 Americans lost their lives in this attack, and just under 2,000 were wounded. It was almost unbelievable. We, the British, almost in the same breath were now at war with Japan, and the official declaration followed without delay. At last our greatest ally was with us, and both our countries were now up to the neck in this Second World War. President Roosevelt was now able to harness the American nation together in a huge chain of action. Winston Churchill knew in his heart this would eventually bring us a united victory, no matter how bad the situation appeared to be at the time, and however long it would take. America would now concentrate on replacing lost naval vessels and enlarge their navy as quickly as possible. Overall armament production for their own forces became a top priority. We ourselves needed to maintain the flow and increase supplies for our own forces, as well as diverting

95

supplies from our own programme to Russia. Much thought was applied to these many problems.

The sudden severity of the war at this time was so great it was decided that Winston Churchill, Lord Beaverbrook and key commanders of our forces should for the second time visit President Roosevelt in Washington without delay. The first visit had been in early August, when Churchill and his party had voyaged on the battleship *Prince of Wales*, and met Roosevelt in Placentia Bay, Newfoundland. Much was discussed at this historic venue and amongst other things produced the drawing up of the Atlantic Charter by Roosevelt and Churchill, then finally agreed by both governments. This was a most democratic and honourable document, designed for the eventual peaceful existence of mankind after the destruction of the Nazi tyranny. At least it was a good try, and Winston Churchill always believed that one should never give up trying.

On this occasion the return voyage was made via Iceland, where a meeting took place with the regent and the Icelandic cabinet. A parade of British and American forces was inspected and the new airfields being constructed were also viewed. Churchill noted that the celebrated hot springs in Iceland were used in a small way for heating and he suggested they should be used for heating the whole of Reykjavik – a few years later this was developed. These voyages to America seemed to be of high risk for such important leaders to take. Long distance air travel for a group of VIPs at the time was out of the question, and these high-level meetings with our powerful ally were vital.

For this second voyage on 12 December, 1941, Churchill and his team set forth to the Clyde to join the newly completed battleship *Duke of York*. This great vessel, with its passenger list of British leaders aboard, would be escorted by a flotilla of British warships.

The convoy planned to make an average speed of twenty knots for the whole voyage, covering the necessary evasive tactics expected. As the ships sailed through the Bay of Biscay, the weather worsened. They had to cross the U-boat stream which ran in and out of the French ports used by the Germans for attacking Atlantic shipping. The weather became very rough and this important British flotilla had to slow down to some six knots in the heavy seas. The Admiralty had instructed the captain of the *Duke of York* not to leave the escorting flotilla, but Admiral Pound, the First Sea Lord, old sea dog and great friend of Winston's among the company aboard, had other ideas about U-boats and speed – like putting one's foot down. So that's what was done – full power my hearties, and the great ship leapt forward, leaving the flotilla behind, plunging through the waves in the pitch black night with hatches battened down, making the best speed possible, until fresh escorts met them from the Azores… and then eventually sailed the pond safely.

There was some concern that the Americans might need to divert most of their main armaments production for their own requirements, which would leave us dangerously short of vital supplies. However, Lord Beaverbrook had considered the overall situation based on previous knowledge, and was convinced the Americans would meet the challenge. That advice was the tonic that Churchill needed at this critical time.

One of the main subjects discussed at the highest level was the volume of armaments and aircraft needed for the British forces to maintain the war against Hitler in all theatres, and I guess there must have been a figure added to meet the new threat coming from Japan.

On 28–29 December Churchill travelled by train to Ottawa to stay with Lord Athlone, the Governor-General. On the 29th there was a meeting of the Canadian War Cabinet. Following this the Prime Minister, Mackenzie King, introduced Churchill to the conservative opposition, with whom he discussed at length the overall hostilities and problems that existed. They were keen and full of support. On the 30th he addressed the Canadian parliament, which still had relations with the Vichy government in France, which could become extremely helpful in the future of the war – a strange and useful situation where we could one day bring France back into the democratic circle and away from the overriding German dominance. Vichy was still not officially at war with the United Kingdom, and they still had some limited naval resources such as the fleet at Toulon. These ships had already clashed with British and Free French forces, which was an uncomfortable nightmare for all concerned. Churchill also explained to the Canadians how he saw the progress of the war developing and how the allies would build up their strength with the huge production programme being planned by the Americans, strongly aided by the Canadian programme. The considerable setbacks being experienced at the time would, he believed, be overcome stage by stage, and in so many words he said that nothing would deter the allies from their final goal.

He had been very well received by the Canadians and finally returned to Washington. Top-level meetings with the Americans finally drew to a close and on 14 January, 1942 Winston Churchill bid farewell to President Roosevelt, with whom an even closer bond had been formed.

The British group then flew to Bermuda, where the *Duke of York* was lying at anchor with its escorting destroyers. The aircraft which had carried them was one of America's new giant Boeing flying boats, a huge aircraft with two decks. Churchill became very impressed with this great flying machine. The thought that they needed to get back to the UK as quickly as possible in the disturbing war-torn situation that confronted him sparked the seeds of a change of plan for the return voyage. 'Why not fly home?'

At the time, flying across the Atlantic was considered to be too much of a risk for an important governing group to take. There were few aircraft suitable for the 3,500–mile journey to carry the key members of the British party in one hop... but would this great new flying boat be the answer? After arriving in Bermuda, Churchill approached the captain of the flying boat and put the question, did the first pilot, Captain Kelly Roberts, think the great flying boat could fly just six key members of the British party back to the UK in one hop? The captain's reply was in the affirmative. With reduced baggage, a full load of fuel and with a favourable weather forecast which indicated a tail wind of 40 mph, they would fly the 3,500 miles in around twenty hours. The experienced captain was fully confident. It must be appreciated that air speeds and cruising altitudes were much lower in 1942 compared with present-day performances.

Churchill then approached Air Chief Marshal Portal and the

First Sea Lord, Admiral Pound. At first they turned the idea of flying down, but then with Churchill's explanation of the urgency, and that all three, plus Beaverbrook, Field Marshal Wilson and Colonel Hollis, would all get back home quickly to get on with some very urgent planning, they became convinced. They should grab the opportunity – after all U-boats were still capable of sinking battleships! The die was cast. The remainder of the British party, with full luggage and records would return on the *Duke of York*.

In the afternoon Churchill addressed the Bermuda Assembly, pressing the point that we should give the Americans their full support in establishing the US naval and air bases in the island. This had already created some unrest amongst local politicians. However, with the explanation that the whole of the British Empire was now at stake in this terrible war, they acquiesced.

On the following day, 15 January, all was made ready, and in the afternoon Churchill and his colleagues joined the flying boat by launch in the harbour. Captain Kelly Roberts had warned that the take-off would be somewhat ponderous, with a full load of fuel plus other factors. They taxied out to the fullest extent of the harbour. Throttles were opened wide – it seems that they all gripped their seats as the great flying boat took some time to become unstuck. They lifted about a quarter of a mile from the reef, and then cleared the low hills with a few hundred feet to spare.

They cruised at a height of some 7,000 feet at an indicated air speed of around 135 mph plus a 40 mph tail wind. There was good service in the dining room and the lounge. Churchill had a large bedroom in the stern which doubled as a bridal suite in better times.

Just before dawn, Churchill went up to the flight deck and sat in the co-pilot's seat for an hour, and he admitted that he felt anxious. They had already flown for ten hours through cloud and mist and had only had sight of one star in that time, so they could well be somewhat off course. They could not use radio transmission and had to rely on dead reckoning, which could not be corrected without sightings. Hours later, towards the end of their ETA, they should have already snatched a sight of the Scilly

Isles. A discussion took place and Lord Portal and the captain made a decision – they immediately turned north and in the following thirty minutes through the broken cloud they sighted the English coastline, and were soon over Plymouth, and splashed down safely, to everyone's relief.

Later it was revealed that if they had stayed on their original course for another five minutes they would have been over the German ack-ack guns in Brest. As it was, their final flight path was the same as that used by enemy aircraft coming in from Brest. The large flying-boat had been picked up by radar and reported as an enemy aircraft. They were not expected to fly in from this direction. Six Hurricanes had been scrambled to attack an enemy aircraft. Fortunately they did not find their quarry, and returned to base.

Whilst Churchill and his party had been away in America, many situations had developed in various theatres. Continuous reports had been sent to them to keep them fully informed of the overall situation. Dates in this saga will therefore overlap in several areas during the American visit.

The Japanese were already fighting in China and they now turned their attention to Indo-China. Their eyes were then on Malaya and the Dutch East Indies. They wanted land for expansion and oil. They sat watching world events and waited for opportunities. At this time the Japanese almost had a free hand to pick and choose where they would strike next.

Around this same period more black news followed for the British. German U-boats had now established a force in the Mediterranean and sank the *Ark Royal*. A short time later the battleship *Barham* was torpedoed and capsized. Then on 18 December, at night, an Italian submarine released three underwater torpedo contraptions, each one controlled by two frogmen, who positioned and attached their time bombs beneath the battleships *Queen Elizabeth* and *Valiant*. These were timed to detonate on the morning of the 19th. Both ships were badly damaged. The six men had penetrated the harbour of Alexandria when the boom gates opened to allow the passage of shipping. In just a short time much of the British eastern battle fleet in the Mediterranean was either sunk or put out of action for a long time.

On the same day as the disaster in Alexandria harbour, information was received in Malta that an important enemy convoy was approaching Tripoli with much-needed supplies for Rommel. Immediately, Naval Force 'K' in Malta, consisting of RN cruisers *Neptune*, *Aurora* and *Penelope* and four destroyers, was despatched to attack the enemy convoy. As this force approached Tripoli, they unfortunately sailed straight into a new enemy minefield, with disastrous results. *Neptune* was badly damaged and the other two cruisers also sustained some damage, but were able to get away. The destroyer *Kandahar* then went into the minefield to rescue the crew of the *Neptune* which was drifting, but she too struck a mine and was badly damaged. The *Neptune* still drifting hit two further mines and finally sank. Only one man from the crew of some 700 survived. As for the *Kandahar*, she remained afloat and eventually drifted out of danger. The destroyer *Jaguar* found her the next night and saved most of her crew.

And so the Italian convoy carrying supplies for the German forces in Tripolitania got through. Rommel and his Panzers needed these supplies very badly after their defeat by General Auchinleck.

With the sinking of a further cruiser, *Galatea* by U-boat, the British Naval Force 'K' operating from Malta was now non-existent. In truth the Royal Navy had almost vanished from most of the Eastern Mediterranean, apart from a few destroyers and three cruisers from Admiral Vian's squadron. It was indeed a black period for the British naval forces in this area. Additionally two capital ships, the *Repulse* and *Prince of Wales*, were also lost in the Far East, which added to our problems. Both ships were sunk by aerial attack using torpedoes and bombs. This situation was kept quiet as long as possible for obvious reasons.

After the Japanese success at Pearl Harbor using bombs and torpedoes, and Hitler's success using dive bombers to spearhead his army's advance in Europe, it is clear that small fast aircraft in large numbers, flying at low level, loaded with bombs and torpedoes, proved themselves time and time again on land and sea – a lesson the allies had to quickly learn.

Japanese history makes interesting reading. Winston Churchill pointed out how both Britain and America had influenced the transition of Japan from a middle age culture to a modern culture in just two generations, but unfortunately retaining much of its past customs. Already, to the surprise of the Western nations, they had defeated Czarist Russia in 1905 on land and sea. They had fought with us in the First World War and kept the Germans out of the Far East, but in this second World War they had sided with the Germans. This was more to do with convenience and thinking this would play into their hands to win more territory. By the end of 1941 their industrial base had become modern and they had built a large strong disciplined army and a modern navy and air force. The ancient Japanese culture and thinking was now somehow split between the old and the new. The mixing of the warrior spirit of the samurai and the modern fighter pilot produced the one-way ticket of the reckless kamikaze attacks, believing these acts would bring great spiritual rewards in the afterlife with their ancestors.

There was no doubt now that with the loss of a large part of the American Pacific Fleet in Pearl Harbor and the loss of our two capital ships in the Pacific, the Japanese would next strike somewhere in Malaya. Already Hong Kong had been attacked by a large Japanese force on the same day as the attack on Pearl Harbor. The siege lasted from 7 December until Christmas Day, when the garrison under Major General Maltby could hold out no longer. It was a brave resistance as they knew there was no hope of any aid reaching them. They fought at point blank range, backed up with 2,000 civilians in the Volunteer Defence Corps, and just six battalions of the standing army, two of which were Canadian. They had a small number of mobile artillery and limited coastal and anti-aircraft guns defending the port. The Japanese attacked with a large force of three divisions with supporting aircraft. Both sides suffered heavy casualties, but the enemy with their overwhelming numbers were unstoppable. The brutal medieval streak in the Japanese treatment of prisoners was strongly evident.

The tentacles of the Japanese invasion had spread alarmingly, and in the same period they landed on the Malay peninsula, where we had some airfields with limited forces. These were quickly overpowered. They then attacked Kota Bharu farther south along the peninsular, protected by a British infantry brigade covering beach defences for thirty miles. The Japanese had a whole division which tried landing along this stretch of coast. The British defenders held them back for a time, supported by some limited air cover. Heavy casualties were inflicted upon the invaders. Our forces after three days were again eventually overwhelmed by numbers, also taking heavy casualties, and were finally ordered to withdraw southwards.

The enemy had now established themselves on several airfields. In the meantime some Dutch submarines farther north had sunk some Japanese shipping, which helped to slow the advance a little, but the enemy was so numerous their attack could not be held back for long.

By the middle of December 1941 the surge of Japanese forces along the Malay peninsula looked extremely menacing, and thoughts had emerged that even Burma and India could be in their plan of expansion. Penang had been overrun by 17 December.

The Australian government had by now become extremely anxious about the progress of the Japanese. Many of their best troops were already in other theatres and the long coastline of Australia would be difficult to protect in the event of an attack. They felt that Singapore should have been better protected, but of course all our strength had been used to resist the German and Italian aggression in Europe and North Africa. Also large quantities of armaments had been diverted to the Russian front, being a vital strategic priority for the downfall of the Nazi menace. There had also been some criticism from some ignorant elements in Westminster at the time, but eventually Churchill asked for a vote of confidence, which was given him.

There was little doubt that the campaign to fight the Japanese as they advanced towards Singapore was poorly planned. There was an attempt to slow down the enemy by holding them around Johore, but despite reinforcements arriving in the area the plan failed and the forces were fragmented. The Japanese strategy in jungle warfare was well planned and their numbers attacking from different directions overcame our tired and battle-worn troops. Although our soldiers, including many Australians, Indian and Malayan brigades put up stiff resistance against a clever and cunning enemy, the result was a foregone conclusion.

At the time, the enemy had command of the air and also had acquired many small boats and craft to attack and infiltrate along the unprotected west coast of the peninsula. Our diminished Navy had only a few light craft, some quickly converted with light arms to stop the enemy's infiltrating strategy along the coast. These brave attempts in daylight were quickly sunk by Japanese low-flying strafing attacks.

Our resisting forces were inexperienced in the jungle warfare which was necessary along the peninsula. Additionally, our airfields were poorly protected and the available aircraft were few, and most were of inferior performance. At a later stage several shipments of Hurricane aircraft arrived by different routes, but a number were damaged in transit. The aircraft were urgently used as they became available, which created a situation where our pilots were consistently outnumbered. It was a brave attempt, but with the large number of enemy aircraft losses eventually overtook them.

Ultimately, with the airfields about to be overrun, the remaining aircraft were flown to Sumatra. What followed was a brave, reckless story. The overall campaign was under the supreme command of General Wavell, who covered the whole of North Africa and the Far East. He was well aware of the limited resistance that could be made against the Japanese, as he had visited Singapore on 10 February 1942, before the final collapse. His commanders on the spot had kept him fully informed of the complete situation.

A plan had been prepared to evacuate some 3,000 key personnel to Java, including technicians, surplus staff officers, nurses and others who would be needed to carry on an organised resistance against the enemy. With this group went Air Vice Marshal Pulford and Rear Admiral Spooner, who had been in command of the air and naval forces. Further tragedy followed. Some eighty small vessels of all kinds which had left Singapore on the 13th and 14th carrying this group, were attacked by a Japanese naval force which was escorting an enemy expedition to attack Sumatra. Most of the little ships were either sunk or captured.

It was only after the war that the story of this tragedy was revealed. On 15 February 1942 the vessel carrying Air Vice Marshal Pulford and Rear Admiral Spooner, plus some forty-five personnel, was attacked by enemy destroyers and driven ashore on a small island. Some native crew were killed and some dispersed. What happened next is a bit sketchy, but they had a bad time. A New Zealand officer and a small group eventually prepared a native boat to sail to Batavia for help. After seven days of tropical storms they successfully arrived in Batavia (Djakarta), and raised the alarm for their comrades. By now there was much unrest in Java, but they did succeed in arranging an attempted rescue. Unfortunately, this failed.

Of the two senior commanders, Pulford and thirteen others died from tropical conditions and diseases before the end of March, and Spooner and three others died in April. On 14 May the only other senior surviving officer in the group, Wing Commander Atkins, realised there was no hope, so he and seven others sailed to Sumatra in a native boat and were captured by the Japanese. They were then taken back to suffer in a prison camp in Singapore.

It became painfully obvious that the enemy was too strong, and our forces could not hold out for long. All equipment and dockyards were ordered to be destroyed or made unusable. There was much hardship and alarm with an impending shortage of water. Food stocks were getting low, and there was very little petrol. General Percival, the senior commander on the spot, was aware that the troops were utterly exhausted and were physically incapable of launching a counter-attack. When all hope of resistance had gone and with General Wavell's previous agreement that further bloodshed was pointless in such circumstances, General Percival decided on capitulation. On 15 February 1942 at 8.30 p.m. the Japanese demanded and received unconditional surrender.

Churchill received a most comforting message from President Roosevelt upon learning of the fall of Singapore. In so many words, he assured Churchill and the British people of his thoughts, and the offer of any help needed in these trying times. It was a message from a most kindly and generous human heart, and a most powerful and trusted ally.

Many years later after the war, in 1980, I met an accountant, Stanley Buckle by name, who, when yarning about the war years gradually unfolded his own personal story to me of when he had escaped from the horrors of Singapore in the last days of the collapse.

Stan was on the ground staff of the RAF. When he was a boy he had contracted polio, which had affected one leg. In his adult life this left him with one weak leg. When he was conscripted he was taken into the RAF, and as far as I understood was in radio and telecommunications. Eventually he was shipped out to Singapore.

When the collapse of our forces came, Stan said everything went wild. He did not see a single British aircraft, and the Australian troops were frantically trying to get to the docks or jetties. Stan somehow got in the rush with his weak leg and scrambled onto a paddle steamer, which pulled away at the poor rate of knots which such craft attain even when at full power. The Japanese had brought along some small mobile artillery, and the paddle steamer was soon hit and promptly started to sink. Stan was flung into the water. A great lump of wood went floating by, which Stan managed to grab, and he started to float away in the current.

Whatever the time span, it seemed like hours and hours to Stan, and also there were probably sharks in these waters. Quite suddenly, a ship came into view just as Stan was starting to give up hope – lo and behold it was an Australian destroyer looking for survivors. He was taken to Australia and eventually shipped back home.

Chapter Seven
UP AND AWAY

It was some five months after attestation that I received my papers from the RAF. I was required to report for aircrew training on 27 April 1942 to the Air Crew Receiving Centre, Regents Park, London.

I was one of a new intake, and we were housed in some flats situated a short distance from the zoological gardens. My group was very soon marched off to get fitted out with uniforms. A small white flash was supplied to position in the front of our forage caps to indicate that we were aircrew under training.

The restaurant in the zoological gardens had been taken over and had become our dining hall, with much amusement and wisecracks. Whilst eating our meals, one could hear the whoops of animals and large captive birds which gave a remote holiday atmosphere to the surroundings.

These brief relaxing moments were quickly dispelled when our drill corporal, by the name of Gaffney, arrived on the scene. Corporal Gaffney's job was to put us through a piece of drill discipline to show that we were now no longer civilians and had to bow to his commands. Drill corporals and sergeants (and no doubt Corporal Gaffney was a drill sergeant in waiting) were a breed of love/hate characters. He was a rather small Glaswegian, who had a ferocious streak which came to the surface when he marched us to the dining hall. Although our flat was a short distance from the zoo, it was far enough to bring us to our knees when Gaffney marched our squad at a speed two or three times faster than any other squad. In fact all the other squads soon had a name for us – 'Gaffney's Greyhounds'. It was painful, but somehow hilarious. Gaffney wanted to make us the smartest squad in the whole unit. Possibly he was after some promotion. However, when he was away from the drill or marching routine he became quite human and almost friendly.

The squad in our flat came from all walks of life, and even from different countries, but all had the same ambition: to become pilots in the RAF. We came under the heading of RAF/VR (Volunteer Reserve) for the duration of the war. If one came from a country other than the UK, a short flash bearing the name of the country became available and was usually positioned at the top of the sleeve of the uniform. This could produce some odd clusters of multinational characters on occasions. There was one fellow in our flat who came from Bermuda. He was white and the story was that his father owned Bermuda Airport. This in 1941 would have meant a fairly free and easy lifestyle.

At this stage of my life, if ever I became a pilot I would have graduated from a BSA bicycle with a Sturmey Archer three-speed hub gear to a Tiger Moth. Our friend from Bermuda, however, was quick to tell us that he had already put in some hours flying 'Cats', that being the way-out laid back terminology for Catalina flying boats – that is for those with some experience. This was all in keeping with a tropical paradise with plenty of water, so up to a point it rang true. It emerged eventually that he was more of a passenger getting the chance to hold the controls of an aircraft once in a while because he lived virtually on an airfield which his father owned.

Catalina aircraft came in two versions – a flying boat or the amphibious version with a retractable undercarriage, ideal for such a location. Our friend, of course, by his own account was also somewhat of a ladykiller – and the girls were putty in his arms. Glimpses of this blissfully exaggerated lifestyle went down well with the boys with some amusement, and broke up the moments of monotony waiting for something to happen.

In due course we were assembled to get overseas injections for the tropics. This separated the men from the boys – some of our intrepid brethren actually passed out, or nearly so, when the needle of rather large dimensions was plunged into the anatomy. Technology was not quite so advanced in those days. So we were going abroad, but where?

Eventually, our stay in Regents Park came to an end. We were posted to a unit in Brighton for two weeks to be fitted out with flying kit. We managed some walks along the front. There was very little to do but wait and write the odd letter home. Looking back, we had become part of a big drive to train young men to fly and to build a much larger Air Force to cover many different theatres. There were a number of training areas where we could be sent – the USA, Canada, the Union of South Africa and Southern Rhodesia.

Very soon we were on our way to West Kirby to await our ship. This resulted in a further period of boredom, but obviously careful preparations were going on in the background to assure a safe grouping of ships in our convoy for a voyage through some dangerous waters. At this stage we thought very little about such matters, but there were many questions in our thoughts as to where we were bound.

Finally on 26 July 1942 we embarked on our ship, the HMT *Rangitiki*, which before being commissioned as a troopship had served as a New Zealand refrigerated meat transport of some 17,000 tons. She was quite a large ship and our quarters for the duration of the voyage were a wide open-plan area with portholes along the port side. Long bench-type tables were arranged across the width of the deck where we ate our meals and passed the time. Above our heads were rows of hooks, which had originally been used for hanging frozen carcasses of lamb. As a troopship these hooks were used for hanging our hammocks at night. During the daylight hours we could promenade around the deck. We could not visit other decks unless for some specific reason, such as a lecture on aircraft recognition or stars in the night sky, etc. We were envious of the group of fully-fledged pilots on the deck above. We knew not where they were bound, as we had no contact.

At this time we held the lowest possible rank in the Air Force – untrained AC2 – and we were treated sometimes like serfs, which brings me to the memory of a most distressing task which was suddenly thrust upon me. With the large number of servicemen on board ship, it was necessary for food supplies to be moved from storage on a regular basis. Some supplies were stored in the very bottom of the hold. We had not thought much about this until one day the occupants of my table found to our dismay that we were not on a holiday cruise, and that it was our turn to move supplies from storage to the galley.

We were led on a trek deep down to a low point in the bowels of the ship. There was some light, but it was gloomy. Very little was said, and I found myself being directed towards the base of an extremely long ladder rising upwards towards an unloading area, which seemed a long way heavenwards. As I reached the bottom of this ladder, a very large sack of wet slippery onions was thrown over my left shoulder and I was directed up the ladder.

The weight of the sack was uncommonly heavy, and every step upwards with this soggy mass weighing me down produced a frightening sensation. The higher I rose the more the ladder joined in the movement. My immediate thought was that if I slipped it would be the end. However, there was only one way to go and that was upwards. Slowly I managed to get into the rhythm and finally made the loading bank. The sense of achievement replaced the fear. It was a large ship and thankfully that was the only time we were called to move the ship's stores.

An American in our group named Develin, who would have worn a USA flash on the sleeve of his uniform tunic, turned out to be a New York newspaper reporter. He was still preparing clippings of news for his paper. It appeared that many Americans at this time had opted to join the RAF although they were already at war themselves following Pearl Harbor.

Our convoy ploughed on, running down the west coast of Africa. We had two old Polish vessels in the convoy which we understood were coal burners and which at times reduced the convoy's speed down to some eight or nine knots. Our destroyer escort sometimes sped between the ships, presumably keeping a tight check on U-boats.

Dramatically we suddenly had a serious happening, and as far as I can remember it was some time before we arrived in Freetown. There was no log available for we AC2 untrained servicemen to refer to, but the actual happening is still crystal clear in my mind.

A Short Sunderland flying boat approached the port side of the *Rangitiki*, flying quite low, below 1,000 feet. Suddenly our gun, which most troopships carried for protection, opened up.

Many of us were on deck at the time taking air. The nose of the Sunderland rose momentarily and then dropped like a great dead bird, plunging vertically into the sea, completely disappearing into the depths. It was sudden, quick and almost unbelievable. A destroyer rushed down through the convoy, appearing to pass directly over where the Sunderland had dived in, and flashed a lamp signal back in morse code, which one or two wireless operators on deck read as 'Regret no survivors'. Our convoy pressed on.

We were all very disturbed. Then, shortly after, the story passed through the ship stating that the Sunderland had given the 'wrong signal for the day'. No matter what the aircraft looked like, and as convoys are so vulnerable, action is immediate if the wrong code is given. Also it was rumoured that the Germans had captured one or two Sunderlands and were using them to attack convoys. We understood that a court of enquiry was underway, but the full story was never officially released to us

Our convoy stopped in Freetown to take on fresh water and whatever other items ships required. Native boys swam out to where we were moored in the harbour and gave their performance of diving for coins in water where large sharks could be seen swimming at some distance. The tropical landscape seen from the deck of the *Rangitiki* was a new horizon for my eyes. One of our group, a lad named Tilbury, obtained permission to go ashore to meet his father, who was a soldier stationed in Freetown. Sadly, some months later, Tilbury was killed in a flying accident, and I was one of the pall-bearers at his funeral.

Shortly afterwards, we sailed onwards on the last leg of our journey, and by now we were aware that we were heading for training in southern Africa. Here we could learn to fly in a peaceful sky away from the harassment of enemy activity.

The heat on board ship was at times suffocating on this voyage, and portholes had to be closed at night to keep the ship in total darkness. At times it was almost unbearable trying to sleep in the suffocating heat, and a few of us would steal up to the open deck in the middle of the night when all was quiet, clasping our emergency life-savers, which also unofficially became a makeshift pillow. I would sometimes attempt to lie on top of a deck locker, but it was really too short in length. When this became unbearable I would curl up under the gun mounting, which was quite a large space but if the gun had suddenly fired would have been somewhat nerve-racking. Eventually after a cooling-off period on the open deck with sea breezes we would creep back to our deck quarters, which at night resembled a sea of hammocks. Finding one's own hammock from beneath when half asleep became a somewhat difficult exercise.

Unfortunately, after a few days the so-called fresh water taken on in Freetown started to give the occupants of our deck acute diarrhoea, and no doubt the rest of the ship suffered likewise. The standard treatment for this was a short course of opium tablets, which completely reversed the malady to the extreme, causing a bout of constipation. Oh boy, what a cruise this turned out to be! We showered in seawater, which after a few weeks led to a salty scalp and a marked stiffening of the coiffure, which produced some strange appearances.

Eventually, the convoy settled down to a continuous boring routine of overheated nights amongst the hammocks and a warm sea breeze by day. Flying fish became a fairly common sight as we plunged onwards through the waves, eventually crossing the equator. I cannot remember anything special about that as there were so many servicemen on board and this was war. The closeness of danger became apparent later towards the end of our voyage.

As we rounded the Cape on course for Durban we headed into a heavy sea mist, to which we gave little thought. We sailed on with our thoughts about arriving in South Africa and gradually after some time we were out into bright weather. The padre on board ship called a service on the open deck, and gave thanks for our deliverance. The heavy mist had shrouded us from the danger of U-boat attack in the last stage of our journey.

At last we disembarked in Durban on 30 August 1942. The coastal climate was pleasant. Our first impressions of the immediate area was one of complete freedom from any wartime activity. We found that our stay would be short.

The transit camp at which we were billeted was plain and simple, but the lavatory facility was a shock to the system. To this day, I cannot possibly guess who designed it. Was it a Zulu straight out from his kraal, or was it a throwback from a Roman legion? The lavatory installation was built over a large square-shaped miniature running sewer. The complete construction was an approximate ten feet square of solid raw concrete. The height of the square was about eighteen inches. In this were shaped round openings spaced about two feet apart continuously around the edges of the concrete square, directly over the running sewer. This lavatory seating was raw shaped concrete – not battlefield technology under cover, but basic farmyard construction in the confines of a modern town, with a sea front somewhat like Bournemouth. A place of many contrasts.

In our brief stay at this exotic establishment we did manage a short walk along the seafront, which reminded me of a very English promenade, complete with seated windbreaks. In those days apartheid existed, so the occupants of the seafront were mainly white.

We also found time to take a visitor's ride in a Zulu-hauled rickshaw. This was no ordinary rickshaw ride as one might see in Calcutta or the East. It was closer to a Zulu attack on Rorke's Drift. These powerful fellows were dressed in full Zulu habit with headdress and when once they got up speed they would leap in the air between the shafts of the rickshaw and would continue to do this even when running downhill, which was somewhat alarming. Strapping Zulu womenfolk were also a different kind of shock to new arrivals, when seen bouncing through the township wearing little more than strings of coloured beads!

After two days in Durban we moved onwards towards our final destination, which was Bulawayo in Southern Rhodesia. We travelled by narrow-gauge sleeper train from 2 September, via Johannesburg and Mafeking, where we stopped for a short break, announcing that Mafeking had been relieved when finding a modern public toilet adjacent to a statue of Baden Powell. This in a very small town square, close up to the railway station. Thence across the edge of the Kalahari Desert, on to Francistown, Plumtree, arriving in Bulawayo on 3 September, covering a distance of some 860 miles.

Chapter Eight
THE STING AT LAST

Our arrival in Bulawayo was uneventful. We were transferred smoothly from the railway to our first serious training unit together with kit, without incident. This was RAF Station Hillside – ITW (Initial Training Wing).

Southern Rhodesia was still a British colony. At first glance Bulawayo had a faint resemblance to a mid-west cowboy town. Sidewalks were raised up above the level of the compressed earth roadway. The latter was proportionately wide enough for a wagon drawn by a team of oxen to turn around completely and depart in the opposite direction. This had been the layout of the first white settlers, and in appearance nothing had changed, with the exception of the buildings, which were in any case modest constructions.

The area was originally a stronghold of the Matabele people, a main branch of the South African Zulus. King Lobengula ruled from his kraal with ruthless energy, and initially gave Cecil Rhodes the run around until such time as the British Army turned up to keep a semblance of order. I will not attempt to go deeper into history, except to say that when we arrived early in September 1942, over the years Bulawayo had become a simply delightful place. It was clean and efficiently run.

After a few days we had time to explore the immediate area, and found that some kind white middle-aged ladies had done their best to make us welcome, and had a tea room set up and running. There we could sample the delights of ice cream sundaes with locally grown fruits and buttered scones in a typical English pre-war atmosphere – all this where back home air raids continued to plague day-to-day living, and where food was rationed creating severe restrictions on anything vaguely tasty.

Oh yes, our first impressions took our minds off the raging of the Second World War. Our mothers back home had nothing to fear from this kind of reception for their nineteen- to twenty-year-old sons.

Our second impression was that they kept their daughters well locked up, as I cannot remember ever catching sight of a single unattached white girl. At a later stage, we heard that one of our number had become involved with a Rhodesian family. Shortly afterwards, the amorous young blood married the daughter somewhat speedily, before being posted away to climes far away at the end of his training.

The white farmers in the area allowed us to use their clean open-air swimming pool on days off duty, which was much appreciated. The climate was warm and sunny. Southern Rhodesia (now Zimbabwe), being some 4,000 feet above sea level kept the temperature down to a continuously comfortable level. I would rate it as one of the best climates in the world, and it was healthy and mainly free from malaria, although one case did arise during our stay, which was quite unusual.

The town itself had a few shops, all bungalow buildings, and I was surprised to find a Meakers' Gents Outfitters. Sometime later we were able to replace our regulation 'Keystone Copper's topee' with a more worldly planters-type model, which we found was not objected to by our instructors. However, as the climate was barely tropical we frequently wore our blue forage caps with our khaki drill tropical rig with shorts. Slowly we began to feel our feet.

RAF Station Hillside had a simple layout, where open-fronted animal stalls had been thoroughly cleaned and whitewashed, and were used initially as our sleeping quarters with one bed to a stall. A tubular iron spacer marked the width of each stall. This was entirely fresh air open planning, hurriedly prepared, but not at all uncomfortable in a pleasantly warm climate. Separate buildings on the site had been fitted out as lecture rooms, etc.

Not long after we had settled in to this new experience, it became necessary to take part in the protection of buildings around the perimeter of the camp site. It appeared that in the Union of South Africa there was an organisation known as the OBs which was anti-British and preferred to side with the

Germans. This was against the wishes of General Smuts's government, but they made their voice heard and were prepared to travel to Bulawayo and attempt to damage our camp by throwing burning torches on to the inflammable roofing. Our job was to take turns at guarding the outer buildings by patrolling the perimeter with a rifle and bayonet. There was no ammunition and no bolts in the rifles issued, hence the bayonet to give a frightening effect. This was the first time most of us had ever touched a rifle, let alone a bayonet, so it was all a bit of a joke. The OBs never seemed to put in an appearance, and our turn at this exercise was quite brief.

The Initial Training Wing covered instruction lectures on dead-reckoning navigation, compass readings, meteorology and cloud formations, and aircraft recognition, plus some not too irksome physical training. We also had some instruction on aircraft armament and a demonstration with a Browning machine-gun.

Test exercises were given on dead-reckoning navigation by using a protractor and dividers to find the compass course and estimated time of arrival for a flight against a given wind direction, wind velocity and indicated air speed, with the track laid down on a Mercator's projection chart.

In the course of our stay at Hillside Camp I had made good friends with the son of a Darjeeling tea-planter, Garth Crees, who had been to school in the UK, and a Scotsman, Bert Norris from Edinburgh. Towards the end of the course we had a long break. Some went off to the Victoria Falls and some remained in camp, where we revised some background subjects which might make a difference in the final count. We three were all eventually approved to progress to the next stage of training.

During our stay in the immediate Bulawayo area we sometimes killed time when off duty by visiting a small cinema, and after the programme we would stop by a mobile snack bar. This was in fact an old single deck bus with a drop-down side made into a long counter. The owner of this thriving stand-up mobile diner was an industrious Greek. With an RAF station in the vicinity he had a captive clientele – a continuous crowd of hungry young men who would always home in on something tasty in the evening. There were no such things as hamburgers in those days, but his answer was a fresh bread roll filled with a sizzling fried egg and a beaker of steaming coffee. In the still and cool of a Rhodesian sundown it was just the ticket – I bet he became another Lord Forte.

Christmas 1942 at Hillside RAF Station was a great treat for us after the rigours of wartime food rationing back home in the UK. I still hold the menu of the Christmas Dinner to this day, signed by the CO Sqd Leader Abel. This read: Creamed Salmon Patties – Roast Turkey and Bread Sauce – Boiled Ham – Roast and Boiled Potatoes – Green Peas – Christmas Pudding and Brandy Sauce – Mince Pies – Confectionery – Beer – Minerals – Cigarettes – Fresh Fruit – Crackers.

During our whole stay in Southern Rhodesia the food was excellent and built us up to peak condition, which probably was by design.

We found there was no great rush through our flying training. This really resulted in a high level of careful instruction (unlike the beginning of the war when pilots were urgently needed, training was cut to the absolute minimum). By January 1943 we had moved to better accommodation whilst awaiting flying training, to the Kumalo EFTS Pool.

Here we carried on with various activities, including one which was described as a 'Bundu Bash'. Before this took place we were given the odd spot of advice by a local 'white hunter' whom the lads nicknamed 'Snake Bite Sam'. Already there had been a hullabaloo one morning when a green mamba had strayed onto the campsite and was apprehended and killed by a member of the native askari, who then exhibited the dead snake over a branch of a tree. This promptly attracted its mate as mambas apparently travel around in pairs.

The *bundu* is the local term for the bush, or to us the uncivilised landscape. The idea behind this exercise was to give us some experience in travelling rough, if we should ever make a forced landing and had to find our way back to safety on foot. It was a bit like a boy scout's game in exotic country. In this particular twelve-mile exercise, we were grouped in fours. We four friends and other groups were dropped off a truck at intervals along a stripped road, and all had to trek across rough country (the *bundu*) and head for the Matopos Hotel and arrive by early afternoon. Each group was given a map and a prismatic compass.

It would appear that the area was sparsely populated with wildlife, but we had previously noted that the CO's bull terrier 'Simba' at Hillside had a nasty scar on its head after a fight with a leopard.

Our foursome set forth, studiously taking bearings at intervals, finding it not quite so easy as we had anticipated. We made progress around *kopje* (which are Rhodesian hillocks) usually with a tree or large bush at the top, and are scattered all over the *bundu*. These obstructed our sightings with the compass and made it difficult to define an accurate bearing.

We pressed on and soon came across a pathetic little Matabele kraal. A very rough stockade of thin planks and broken tree stumps surrounded the hut, with its badly thatched roof. We could see a little movement inside the stockade but nobody came out as we passed by. It was said that many of the natives suffered from bilharzia, which is the result of a minute parasitic worm which bores its way through the body to the bladder, making the patient very ill and sleepy. This parasite lives on a water-snail which abounds in the natural pools of water occurring in the bundu. The natives bathe in the pools and the parasite transfers from snail to human – a very nasty malady. All pools usually had a warning notice on display and it was also publicised verbally, but the local natives frequently paid no attention to the warning.

Eventually we sighted the Matopos Hotel, after some thirsty work scrambling over some very uneven ground, but not before I nearly stepped on a snake curled up in a cavity. At last our thirst was quenched when we reached civilisation, where a long cool drink was awaiting us at the end of the trek. On another occasion we had a live session of studying the night sky. This entailed sleeping rough with a blanket in the *bundu*, and being awakened at different times through the night to study the movement of the stars. It was not a particularly popular exercise with the lads, but looking back it was an experience and something to remember.

Following various further activities we were given some instruction on the De Havilland Tiger Moth, which we would eventually learn to fly at our Elementary Flying Training School. At this point, we had an unserviceable Tiger Moth in a small hangar which was used only for cockpit familiarisation and general knowledge of the aircraft.

There always have to be characters in a crowd who for some unknown reason wish to take situations into their own hands to prove how different and reckless they are in comparison to the norm – and, of course, we had such a couple amongst our intake. One was Irish and the other American (not our reporter friend on the *Rangitiki*). They were both at the worldly top end of the age bracket in our set, and professed to be keen on a 'shot of Rye'. They probably shot themselves once too often with a South African distillation at the time of the incident – you've guessed it no doubt – they tried out the unserviceable Tiger Moth one evening without permission or instruction on the patch of green outside the hangar. They did not get airborne, and they were not very popular with the CO after the event.

Elementary Flying Training School – 18 February 1943

Ultimately our stay at the Kumalo EFTS Pool came to an end and we moved on to 27 EFTS Induna. We now had much better accommodation. At last we had arrived at a crucial point in our training. If things went very wrong here, we would never get our wings. Most of us in those times had never flown before. Only the rich or the military had this opportunity before the war.

My very first flight in a Tiger Moth gave me both joy and amazement. My instructor was a very experienced pilot, a certain P/O Wright. He was a white South African and a man of advanced years compared with most other instructors. It emerged that he had been a pilot flying the triple-engined Junkers 52 aircraft for a South African Airline, probably carrying both freight and passengers. No doubt there had been a shortage of good instructors and he came into the RAF quickly, which would explain his fairly junior rank.

The Tiger Moth is powered by a De Havilland Gypsy Major motor, developing a maximum of 130 hp. The instructor sits in the front cockpit and the pupil sits in the rear cockpit. There are dual controls and instruments. In those days communication between instructor and pupil was by Gosport tube, which was somewhat primitive but adequate. Speech was naturally windswept. One was completely open to the slipstream and the elements, which initially was a bit startling. Flying goggles and helmet helped to keep eyes from watering and ears from being blown off. We wore one-piece flying overalls, which were adequate for the climate.

There is a particular difference in learning to fly from a ground elevation of some 4,000 feet above sea level, because of the slight difference in air density. The thinner air requires a slightly faster take-off and landing speed, which makes early flying experience more critical than at sea level. It also requires a few weeks for one's body to become adjusted to the higher altitude at ground level. When we first arrived in Southern Rhodesia we were warned that some would experience nose bleeding for the first few weeks. By this time, however, we were all fully acclimatised to these conditions.

In the first lesson, before take-off we went through the layout in the cockpit and how to start the aircraft. This also covered the importance of trimming the aircraft, setting the mixture control to rich for take-off, and tightening the friction nut on the throttle so that it did not slip back.

The Tiger Moth had to be started by a ground crewman swinging the propeller by hand. This involved priming the engine by moving round the propeller, with the two magneto switches off and then calling to the pilot who would confirm by answering, 'Switches off'. After priming came the call 'Switches on' – the pilot would then reply and switch just one switch on. Immediately the ground crewman would swing the propeller forcibly, and as the engine fired the pilot would switch on the second magneto. All was now ready for taxiing out. In this way the Tiger Moth was a bit like flying in World War I; in fact my father used the same jargon when telling me about his own experiences in the Royal Flying Corps when I was a boy.

Once airborne and flying straight and level, in my first flight I was told to put my feet on the rudder pedals and to hold the

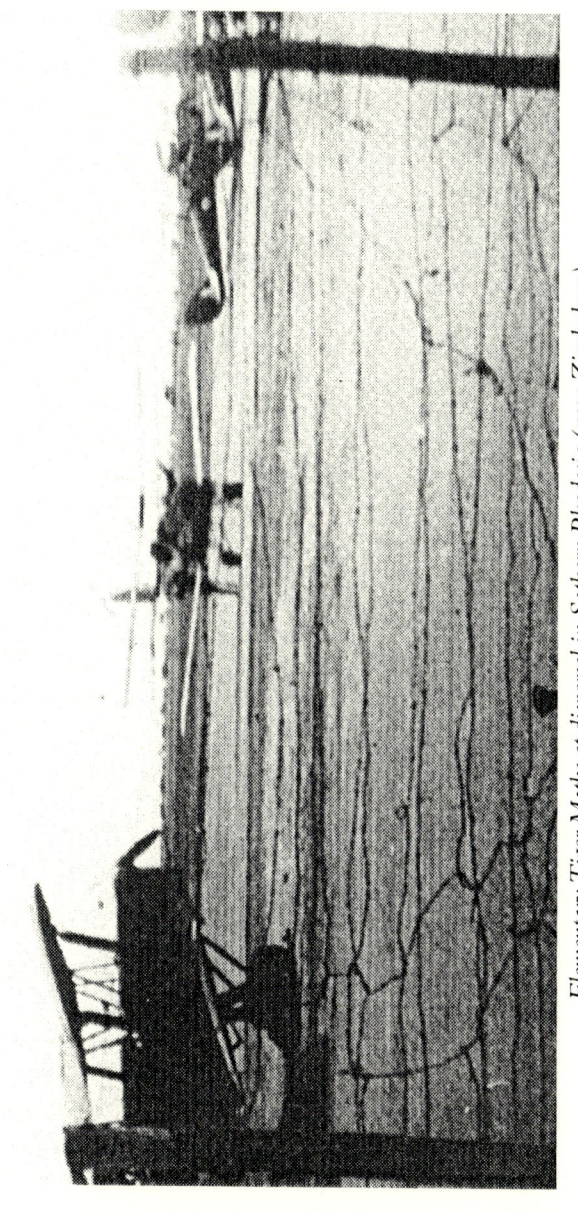

Elementary Tiger Moths at dispersal in Sothern Rhodesia (now Zimbabwe)

control column (joystick). P/O Wright then said to me, 'Have you flown before?' I replied 'No sir.' He then said that most pupils grab the controls too vigorously, 'And stop calling me sir.' I immediately liked this instructor.

The second flight followed on the same day. This time, broadening the experience, the effect of controls, flying straight and level, maintaining height without yawing. And so each day the lessons progressed – taxiing, taking off into wind, climbing, gliding, medium turns, spinning to left and right, gliding approach and landings – and then a change took place.

After the skilled instruction of P/O Wright I was passed over to a Sergeant Lescure, presumably to get me off solo. This young sergeant was a qualified pilot, but I had no idea of his background. I was beginning to feel very unhappy – there had already been a cull of some trainees, notably some rather large fellows. These would eventually be passed on for training to become observers (later to be called navigators) or wireless operator/air-gunners.

My own instruction via Sergeant Lescure continued unabated. He was concentrating on landings, so he would fly the aircraft around the circuit and say 'You've got her' on our final approach just before touchdown, and would then suddenly take the control back before landing and we would go around again, and again, and again. I became very disturbed at this technique, but could not argue with my instructor. I began to feel that if I did not go solo soon I would be scrubbed. Perhaps they had forgotten me. Suddenly there was a change of tactic. Just one lesson was given me by a different instructor. Then my favourite instructor, P/O Wright, who had now gone up a rank to F/O Wright, casually walked up to me on the same day and asked how I was getting on. To this I opened up and said what I thought of Sergeant Lescure's technique, as I wanted to feel more of the aircraft in flight before making an approach and landing.

Without more ado I took off once more with F/O Wright and at the end of the lesson landed – he immediately unstrapped, got out and told me to go solo, just one circuit. I was so overjoyed I took off and powered round in a big sweeping arc and made quite a respectable landing. Tiger Moths, being small, light biplanes, tend to float around, and although easy to fly one could say they are difficult to fly really well. As my wheels touched and lifted slightly, I settled with a short burst of throttle. I taxied back. F/O Wright walked up and said 'I liked the touch of throttle as you landed, but what about that regulation circuit' – which was a rather staid affair, making 90° turns at each corner of the circuit. My effort had been fired with enthusiasm and excitement – I felt I had let myself be carried away with joy, which was wrong – but he just gave me a smile, and I was over the hump.

Following my first solo, I returned to Sergeant Lescure for instruction and had no further problems. There is no doubt that being an instructor is no easy job, and at times only experience can produce the right decision.

The circuit at Induna was at times extremely busy, and we trainee pilots often referred to this as Piccadilly Circus. One had to keep a good lookout for other Tiger Moths, particularly on one's approach. We were not in touch with ground control by radio, as all airfields are today. The only contact was by signal lamp – green for clear to take off or land, and red for no permission.

Added to the hazards was a rather large hill raised up like a huge boulder, something like 300 feet high (as far as I can remember), and not far from the circuit – named Thabus Induna. For the Matabele this was the 'meeting place of the headmen'. King Lobengula, in far off days, would hold court for wrongdoers, and if they were found guilty without more ado they would be hurled off the top.

During our flying instruction at Induna we were all eventually given a few flying lessons by a certain flight commander, who had to my mind the uncanny characteristics and rotund appearance of Hermann Goering. I believe he was also a South African, but had a totally different attitude to teaching. My friend Garth Crees had already warned me of this instructor's temperament, following his own experience. It was also said that one pupil found to his dismay that during a flying lesson our portly flight commander had removed his own control column, unstrapped himself, turned round facing the pupil and waved his stick in a menacing manner because the pupil had not closely followed his instructions. The story did the rounds and joking comments were made saying that a slow roll was the only answer to this kind of behaviour.

Training proceeded with different instructors, and solo flights continued to increase. Instruction covered flying exercises of every description, steep turns, low flying, climbing turns, forced landings, spinning, side slipping etc. Dispersed between our flying instruction we also commenced indoor Link Training. This was in support of instrument flying, by use of a completely enclosed electro-mechanical-pneumatic model of an aircraft cockpit, which had full flying instruments, flying controls and movement in a static indoor housing. Most flying courses in the RAF at this time were usually backed up with a number of hours of Link Training practice. This was necessary for full instrument flying training and experience, but was not particularly popular amongst we trainee pilots.

Eventually it became my turn to have a flying lesson with our turbulent flight commander. I felt distinctly uneasy about this prospect in line with the feelings of most of my comrades. But there it was – Tiger Moth No. 706 was standing in dispersal waiting for 'Hermann Goering' and myself to meet head on. I guessed I should get into the aircraft quickly so as not to keep him waiting. I put on my parachute, clambered into the rear cockpit, strapped myself in and waited.

Suddenly he appeared in a hustle, started to put on his parachute and at the same time said, 'Who told you to get into the aircraft? Get out and wait till I tell you to get in.' Every other instructor at whatever rank would have been happy for the trainee to be already strapped in and ready to go. In this case I had to unstrap, climb out with parachute strapped around me and await his command. When once I was on the ground, he settled himself in and then he turned his head and said 'Now get in.'

This was in fact the first time I had ever made contact with him. I was then told to taxi forward ready for take-off. We got the green signal, and I took off. Things went quite smoothly, much to my surprise, and his only notable comment after each instruction was 'Watch the bubble, watch the bubble.' This is all to do with keeping the aircraft flying accurately without yawing. After thirty minutes we landed and the ordeal had passed. I felt quite pleased with myself for having avoided another mouthful of criticism.

Some time later I had a cross-country test with a certain P/O Nokes. In the middle of this flight the dreaded fine rain and ground level mist called 'gooty', which very occasionally envelops the region without warning, suddenly clamped down on us. These elementary aircraft carried no radio and we were on our own to get out of trouble. P/O Nokes took over and used his considerable skill at low-flying a Tiger Moth at a height of some fifty to sixty feet in a virtual one hundred feet forward visibility, at ground level. Using our compass bearing and picking out trees, he guided us back home safely. Fortunately the slow flying speed of these aircraft just made this performance possible. Although this was an elementary flight it was an experience I shall never forget.

On that same evening it was time to have a session of night flying with the famous scourge of pupil pilots. The weather had cleared and the flare path was illuminated with goose-neck oil-burning flares, which tended to blow out at odd intervals. Somehow we managed to meet at Tiger Moth No. 706 without confrontation and slipped into our respective cockpits in the right order. It was a particularly dark night, and the weaving technique of taxiing towards the taxiing post produced a slight hiccup on my part in the inky blackness lying ahead of the aircraft. The taxiing post had a cross member at the top, with a red light on the left and a green light on the right, representing port and starboard. This was a guide towards the point of take-off for aircraft on an open airfield at night.

I moved slowly forward, swinging the nose to the right and to the left in the approved manner, sitting in the pupil's rear cockpit with the bulk of our flight commander slightly obscuring my line of sight. Straining my eyes for the lights of the post, a small red light suddenly came into view. Briefly, I started to swing the aircraft towards the light, and the menacing voice from the front cockpit exploded about the same instant as I realised my mistake. The light started to move, and the high rear light of a lorry started to move slowly across our path some distance away. I corrected direction slightly and in due course arrived at the right position by the taxiing post.

The lesson lasted for two hours, with night take-offs and landings and general handling. Some take-offs and landings were experienced with goose-necked flares which had blown out, but in all I got away with a reasonably calm session, orchestrated from the front cockpit.

The course continued, with lots of power approaches and landings, precautionary landings, a cross-country test and a forced landing exercise, followed by compass errors and course. As we moved towards the end of Elementary Training there was more night flying, formation flying, aerobatics, instrument flying, spinning and low flying. Finally there came the Chief Flying Instructor's Test by W/Cmdr Amlot, which really cleared us to move on to the next phase of our training. Just one last flight took place with P/O Nokes, which took me through some live instrument flying take-offs, which was good experience. So the first flying course finally ended.

At this point the course would be split between flying single-engined aircraft and twin-engined aircraft. Unfortunately my two friends would go on to fly twin-engined aircraft and I would fly singles. This meant that we would go to different advanced training schools for the rest of our time in Rhodesia.

Service Flying Training School – 1 May 1943

We single-engined lads now moved towards flying more advanced aircraft at 22 SFTS Thornhill, and had now reached the exalted rank of ASU (Acting Sergeant Unpaid). We continued to be paid at a lower rate until we actually won our wings and completed the final part of the course, when we would become full sergeant pilots.

The aircraft we flew initially was the North American Harvard Mark 1, powered by a Pratt and Witney Wasp 550 hp radial engine. This aircraft is well known for its noise due to the direct drive of the propeller shaft. The variable pitch airscrew, wing flaps and retractable undercarriage introduced us to a more advanced specification.

This aircraft, flown from the ground-level elevation of some 4,000 feet above sea level, accentuated its tetchy characteristics. I do not remember having this factor particularly drawn to my attention, but it was stressed that when the aircraft stalled it would flick a wing and quickly go into a spin. If one held off high when landing, the aircraft could under certain conditions flick a wing resulting in a wing tip touching the ground before the wheels, producing what was jokingly referred to as a ground loop – not a very pleasant experience if one should fall into this trap.

Apart from this failing, I found the overall higher performance of the Harvard a great improvement over the Tiger Moth. Every feature made flying a more positive experience. Providing one kept to the safety margins laid down it was a good strong intermediate aircraft to fly. The seating arrangements in the Harvard were the reverse of the Tiger Moth. The pupil now sat in the front cockpit and the instructor in the rear cockpit. The intercom was by microphone and headphones attached to the helmet, which was another great improvement over the Tiger Moth.

Throughout the course we all experienced flying lessons with several different instructors, but the instructor I remember most clearly was Sergeant Clark. He was an Australian from the outback and was a good ten years my senior. It was understood that he was virtually born in the saddle and rode a horse all through his life before joining the Royal Australian Air Force. He was a very careful, reliable and likeable character. He helped me a lot and I looked forward to training sessions with him.

The training exercises were similar to the previous course, but with more performance from the Harvard aircraft. The spinning characteristics of the Mark 1 Harvard were well appreciated and exercises on recovery were practised throughout the course.

One of our number suddenly came to grief in a solo exercise. The young pilot involved was probably flying too low and did not allow sufficient height for recovery – probably from an incipient spin. If one did not pay careful attention to flying speed in any manoeuvre, the Harvard would bite back and could, in some circumstances, take up to 1,000 feet or more to make a full recovery. For this reason we were told to fly at 3,000 feet when practising aerobatics.

There was not much of the machine left in a recognisable

Mark 1 Harvard Aerobatics

condition after this crash, and the remains were put into an open compound for us to see, as a stark warning. This took the wind out of our sails for a time, and we all thought deeply about keeping plenty of height between us and the ground when practising aerobatics.

I and five other ASUs on our course became pall-bearers at our comrade Tilbury's funeral. It was a sad interlude, and it brought home to us that these things happen within the flying fraternity, which create a deep comradeship.

At that time an RAF flying training airfield had a busy and sometimes dangerous airspace, particularly when communication between aircraft and airfield control was limited to signal lamps. On one occasion when Sergeant Clark was at the controls of our aircraft on an approach to the airfield, from my cockpit position I had a downward view. Slightly behind and immediately beneath us, I could see another Harvard making a precautionary approach at the same speed. If we had continued, there would have been a mid-air collision as we reduced height. I quickly warned my instructor and a crash was averted. Neither pilot was in a position to see the situation unfolding. It was only by a quirk of fate that I looked downward rather than forward, which would have been the normal line of sight. I doubt if the crew in the aircraft below ever knew how close to danger they had been.

The course continued with intensity in all areas of flying skills – aerobatics, formation flying, forced landings, spinning, low flying, a night-flying cross-country exercise, high speed stall, night flying with headlamp landings and floodlight landings etc. I had more dual advanced instruction from Sgt Clark (now affectionately known as Cobber Clark), than any other instructor. On 21 June 1943 I had forty minutes of solo aerobatics, and some time later that same day it was my turn to take the final flying test with the Chief Flying Instructor, Sqdn Leader Ogle, for one hour.

Eventually we came to the high point of the test, for which I had been forewarned. This involved a forced landing. Of course we were not expected actually to crash-land the aircraft, but it was not clear in my mind exactly how far we would go. As far as I can remember we were flying around 1,500 feet, when suddenly the throttle lever was yanked back to idling, and the announcement

Mark 2 Harvard

was 'You have engine failure'. We had practised this in our training, and the hope was there would be the necessary factors around in our final test to make a smooth solution for a forced landing. 'Flaps down, undercarriage up for a belly landing – look for reasonably clear area away from trees – wind direction... bonfire smoke... must get in... a bit too high... heavy side slip (I had always fancied side-slipping for some reason)... keep speed up above stall... straighten up... maintain glide straight ahead... ready for belly landing... help! When is this chap going to call it a day?' We were feet from the ground and suddenly we had full throttle and the Sqdn. Leader was climbing away... he certainly judged that to a whisker!

I was so elated that I could not remember the remainder of that flight. At last I had won my wings. In due course we had a short ceremony for the presentation of our wings, and eventually had an entry made in our log books. After all that, we had still not completed our full flying training programme and remained ASUs.

We carried on flying the same aircraft with a concentration of night flying, formation flying, low flying and various odd exercises like taking off out of wind, action in the event of fire, and abandoning aircraft. My friendly instructor Sgt. Clark remained with us up to the end of this final section of our course flying Mk. I Harvards.

We then had a convivial get-together in the mess when it emerged that Sgt Clark would be leaving us, and he would later return to a squadron in North Africa. We said our goodbyes and best wishes.

Advanced Training School, 13 July 1943

We now entered the final part of service flying training with Harvards Mk II and IIA in the Advanced Training School. These machines were smart all-silver versions, slightly less tetchy and they had a better feel about them, particularly when landing. The control knobs were also slightly more upmarket.

Most of our exercises were now involved with ground attack and close support, such as high dive-bombing, low-level bombing and air-to-ground dummy gun attacks. We also had more formation flying, photography, night flying, day cross-country and reconnaissance exercises. At this time flying concentrated much of my thoughts, and the high state of activity made one immune to the thought of danger which could easily creep up in the strangest circumstances. Our training had been thorough and it was just as well.

On 26 July 1943 – it was time for some more night flying. I had completed a one hour dual cross-country night flight with a certain F/O Marshall in Harvard No. 374. Later that same evening I took off solo on a second cross-country night flight in Harvard No. 376. This exercise was a triangular course which returned to base. At the end of the first leg the turning point was easily identified from the chart and by the view at night of the cluster of lights in a small area. There was no blackout at this time in Southern Rhodesia and the stars were clear and bright. African skies can be a picture to behold.

I set course for the second leg, which would take about twenty minutes. Everything was going well. It certainly was a beautiful night sky and the heavens gave a soft glow to the landscape below. I settled down, checked my gyro compass against the magnetic compass and started to peer ahead for my next turning point. Gradually a group of lights came into view. Was this the next turning point? There seemed to be a slight discrepancy; there were more lights a bit farther over – I decided to take a peep at my chart.

To do this I needed to switch on the cockpit light. This light could be angled and had an orange-coloured filter to reduce the glare, which was very necessary. I switched on the light and I was confronted with a white glare full in my face – the orange filter had been removed!

For seconds I was completely dazzled and groped around to turn the wretched light off, but it was long enough for my attention to be taken away from the attitude of flight – suddenly the night sky and stars were in the wrong place and were starting to revolve. For seconds, only seconds I was nonplussed. The Harvard had reverted to its nasty habit and was biting back. I was now in a full vicious spin – at night! Just about a young pilot's worst nightmare.

I had been flying just under 3,000 feet and had lost height rather rapidly. Fortunately our training had been thorough and instinct took over – harsh movements required – stick forward to get the nose down – full opposite rudder – spin stopped – centralise rudder – diving straight at the ground – pulled out – oh boy! was I low. I shall never forget that night. I found myself flying parallel looking down at a railway station platform – the picture is still in my mind's eye of the row of lantern-shaped glass lamps alight along the edge of the deserted platform.

I pulled up into a climb. The noise of the Harvard engine must have awakened a few startled sleepers. I continued to climb and circled the area, firstly to get myself together, and then to set course for base. After that twirl my instruments had toppled. Normally we locked the gyro compass and artificial horizon if practising aerobatics, but this was unplanned; it would take some minutes before they levelled out. I set course for base after I had gained height, using the magnetic compass. I duly arrived back safely, landed and taxied back to dispersal, parked and headed for my room. I met a colleague and mentioned my ghastly night's experience and went straight to bed.

I lay awake still in shock. I realised how close I had been to oblivion. I could not sleep, I prayed. Morning came and I decided to pull myself together. I dressed and there was a knock on my door. It was a friendly character named Poole. He was smiling and said he had heard about my experience the night before and started to apologise. He said at that same turning point he looked at his map, as he was also unsure, and could not see very well with the orange filter, so he decided to take it off – and it was still in the pocket of his flying overall. He had flown Harvard No. 376 the flight before me – he was truly sorry. Of course, taking the filter off himself was not quite the same thing as the unexpected brightness straight in the eyes. How easily a small action when in flight can bring on such a state of chaos!

I never mentioned the subject again, and as far as I know the matter never surfaced – in fact I may have received a black mark for arriving five minutes late back at base on that fateful flight. Ah me!

We continued the course – one high spot was a joint exercise with our friends flying twin-engined Air Speed Oxfords. They flew in towards our airfield and we took off and made interceptions. Unfortunately the flying speeds of the Oxford and Harvard are too close, and it was almost impossible for us to catch and make a close dummy interception. However, the fun side crept in and as R/T was used for the first time 'Tally-ho' could be heard over the air waves as the Harvard's dived towards the Oxfords, but as we straightened out, the gap could not be closed up, particularly if the Oxford pilots opened their throttles.

We continued the remainder of the programme, with operational exercises using live rounds of ammunition for air-to-ground targets and also cine recording for air-to-air attacks. R/T was in use for interceptions and the final exercise was a battle climb in formation.

And so the training period in Southern Rhodesia terminated and I and a number of my comrades found we were being posted to India. Before we departed I was able to meet up again with my old friends Garth Crees and Bert Norris. Garth had already given me an introduction to go and meet his father at the Lopchu Tea Estate in Darjeeling if I ever got the chance. Bert promised that if he ever arrived in London he would travel and see my parents. Garth was to go forward to become a flying instructor in the UK, and it would appear that Bert expected to fly bombers of some type also in the UK.

My 'Indian group' arrived back in Bulawayo en route to Durban, and we received some bad news about our good friend Sgt (Cobber) Clark. He had been killed in North Africa. We had no details of how it had happened. It was for me a sad note, which would leave me with a lasting memory of how I had trained to become a pilot in the RAF with the help of a friendly Australian from the faraway outback, who would never return to his homeland.

Chapter Nine
THE WORLD AT WAR

Whilst my comrades and I had been absorbed in joining the RAF in the UK – then making a voyage to Southern Africa for flying training, followed by our departure for a further voyage to India, the face of the world we knew had changed considerably.

Over the period the war had continued with such ferocity that situations for many had become almost unbearable. The German U-boats had continued to take a huge toll on Allied shipping, and vital cargoes had frequently finished up at the bottom of the ocean. Many lives had been lost and many hearts had been broken.

A Visit to the USA

All through the path of this continuing conflict, our great leader Winston Churchill had steadfastly held on to his belief that the tyranny of our enemies would eventually be overcome. Even when his health was failing, he still led from the front and visited President Roosevelt in America to guide and to consult, so that our two nations could pull together.

Back on 17 June 1942 he had commenced his third wartime visit across the Atlantic, flying with the Chief of the Imperial General Staff and General Ismay for the second visit to Washington, with staff members following by sea. The only way Churchill could fly at the time, because of his health, was at a fairly low altitude, hence the necessity to travel by American Boeing flying boat, which he had already experienced. This had the range to cover the distance, flying at an altitude of some 7,000 feet.

On this particular visit many strategies and situations were studied. Then on 20 June the momentous decision was taken for both our countries to combine research on the atomic bomb with all speed. Prior to this meeting, research on atomic fission had largely been conducted independently. Suddenly it was evident that the race was on as it was believed that the Germans were pressing ahead with their own development, because of their known intent to secure supplies of heavy water. This was a race that the allies could not afford to lose. It was decided the only place to conduct a live test was somewhere in the vastness of America. Both teams would work closely together.

On the morning of 21 June at the commencement of a meeting with President Roosevelt in his study, a telegram arrived which the President glanced at and immediately handed to Mr Churchill. It announced that Tobruk in Libya had fallen, and at least 25,000 men had been taken prisoner. Later it was revealed that the number was considerably more.

Churchill could barely believe his eyes at what he read and immediately asked General Ismay to telephone London for more details. General Auchinleck had previously indicated in so many words that Tobruk was a well fortified stronghold in the desert and would be held, but in fact there had been a difference of opinion amongst some senior officers in the field. It was thought that under certain conditions this was not entirely necessary and resulted in some secondary defences being badly maintained.

Now suddenly a large number of seasoned, mainly South African troops had apparently succumbed to Rommel's smaller but strongly mechanised armoured column. Many of the South African soldiers could not understand why their commanders had given in so easily as they believed they could have resisted and stayed put. This was a great disappointment to General Smuts, who discussed this later with Churchill. The defeat had given our enemy a prized strategic position, plus valuable military supplies, and had strengthened Rommel's hand for a further push towards the prize of Egypt.

This news completely shattered Churchill, and our American friends had immediately seen how deeply it had affected him. It was not only the loss of a strategically important fortress, but also the disgrace he had felt. The stronghold of Tobruk, which had been so hard won, had apparently become so poorly protected in certain areas that at least twice the number of Allied troops than that of the enemy had been trapped and laid down their arms. Roosevelt felt the grave disappointment that Churchill displayed and asked what help they could offer. 'Send us as many Sherman tanks as you can spare,' replied Churchill, and that was what they did. They immediately arranged to transfer 300 tanks, together with some key technical personnel, which was actually being awaited by the US Army. In addition, one hundred self-propelled 105-millimetre guns would follow which could be used for taking German tanks apart.

Churchill and his immediate colleagues then took the return flight to the UK by flying boat on the night of 25 June from the mooring in Baltimore. They then refuelled at Botwood and took off again on 26 June for the flight across the Atlantic via Northern Ireland. They splashed down on the Clyde at dawn on 27 June 1942.

The Desert and Beyond

In the meantime the desert battle was continuing. The New Zealand Division arrived in Matruth from Syria and were quickly moved to high ground on the ridge in the vicinity of Minqa Qaim. Rommel had already broken through an incomplete minefield and encircled the New Zealanders. Their commander, General Freyberg, had been badly wounded, but Brigadier Inglis quickly took over and organised a gallant breakout. Soon after midnight the 4th New Zealand Brigade, with many Maoris in its ranks, moved eastwards and spread out en masse across country and advanced for 1,000 yards without any resistance. Suddenly enemy fire broke out. With fixed bayonets the New Zealanders charged in line. The Germans were taken by complete surprise and were routed in hand-to-hand fighting by moonlight. The remainder of the New Zealand Division struck south east in a sweeping curve, and the whole division was eventually united in Alamein in a high state of triumph after a journey of some eighty miles. In due course they became a strong link in the resistance of the Allied forces which would ultimately break the Axis thrust towards Egypt.

Eventually the planned delivery of US tanks and the separate engines so urgently required rolled off different production lines, and were then shipped in separate vessels for convenience. Unfortunately, the ship carrying the engines was sunk by U-boat. Immediately this became known, a further consignment of engines was efficiently and quickly shipped out by a fast vessel and caught the convoy.

The fall of Tobruk had also created a personal problem for Churchill, amongst the other disasters being experienced at the time. Certain misguided and inexperienced politicians in the British government were again pushing to change the leadership. This had been a very disturbing time for our great leader after all the mental toil and physical effort he had put into keeping our nation afloat. However, this eventually came to nothing. The motion of no confidence was defeated by 475 votes to 25 and the battle in the desert rumbled on.

Certain changes in command for the Middle East which Churchill then introduced after consultation had made things happen. Initially, General Auchinleck was given the job of personally running the desert campaign rather than overseeing his wider responsibilities, where he had relied on other generals to feed him information. This action checked Rommel's advance. More allied troops arrived in the area, and more British aircraft strengthened our forces. Even so Churchill and the High Command found the overall situation so serious that a top meeting was then planned to take place in Cairo.

Immediately Churchill arranged his flight with the aid of a specially modified US long-range Liberator bomber, renamed the Commando. The bomb bay of the aircraft had been opened out and used as extra space for VIPs travelling long distances, and larger fuel tanks were incorporated. The Commando comforts were somewhat spartan in comparison to the Boeing flying boat, but it was a reliable and faster aircraft and highly suited for transporting our vital British leaders in as safe an environment as possible, where landing points were on airfields rather than on water.

This potentially dangerous flight to Cairo was escorted part of the way by four Beaufighters. The young American pilot, Captain

Vanderkloot, who had flown the Commando from America was trusted to take the British party to Cairo by the shorter route. They landed in Gibraltar on the morning of 3 August 1942 and took off at 6 p.m. for the approximately 2,250-mile flight, and avoided dangerous airspaces as far as possible. The Beaufighter escort stayed with them until nightfall. The route took them over Vichy North African neutral territory without incident, eventually flying down the Mediterranean and coastal regions under the cloak of darkness, and they landed in Cairo at dawn on 4 August.

There were many questions to be answered. Had the Desert Army lost confidence in its commanders? To help thrash out this problem and put the Desert Army back into top form, Churchill had called in his trusted advisers – the CIGS; General Wavell, General Smuts from South Africa, the Minister of State for the Middle East, Rt Hon RG Casey, General Brook, General Auchinleck, Admiral Harwood and Air Marshal Tedder.

It was important that the overall Desert High Command should match and outwit the German General Rommel. The Allies had to move fast and turn the tables. Already 300 US Sherman tanks were on the way. Churchill left nothing to chance. He had flown around the desert talking to our soldiers. He finally concluded the troops had definitely lost confidence in their commanders.

This posed some difficult situations. General Auchinleck and his commanders had to be changed or shuffled around. Eventually this was achieved by moving them into different theatres. A somewhat disgruntled General Auchinleck eventually moved farther east to take over a separated Iraq and Persia Command from the previous Middle East Command. Auchinleck was in fact a brilliant strategist, but somehow his grip on the army in the desert had slackened due to the flabby direction of his commanders and generals in the field.

General Alexander became the new Middle East Command supremo. The popular Lieut General Gott was to become commander of the Eighth Army, but sadly he was suddenly shot down when travelling by aircraft and killed. This necessitated further urgent movements of top commanders. After pressure from both Churchill and Smuts when in Cairo, the War Cabinet in the UK reluctantly agreed that General Montgomery should become the new Commander of the Eighth Army and be sent out at once to take up his new post.

Closer Ties with Russia

Whilst these far-reaching events were coming together, Churchill had been preparing for yet another programme of immense importance – a flight to Moscow from Cairo to get closer to Stalin and offer the hand of reason and cooperation to bring down Hitler and his Nazi horde. Joseph Stalin had been pushing his desire for the British to invade German-occupied France across the Channel at once. It was necessary to make the Russians understand the time was not yet right. The Russians themselves were locked in huge battles with the strong mechanised German forces. There were heavy casualties on both sides, so they naturally expected British forces to engage and weaken our joint enemy from a different direction.

Churchill had arranged for American representatives to accompany the British party on this important Russian visit. Eventually, late in the night of 10 August 1942 three planes took off with a party which included War Office staff, American staff, General Wavell (who could speak Russian), Air Marshall Tedder, and Sir Alexander Cadogan. Averell Harriman was the leading American representative sent by Roosevelt, who travelled with Churchill in the same aircraft.

By dawn on 11 August, the flight plan had taken them across the mountains in Kurdistan, and Churchill and his friends in the Commando aircraft found they needed to suck at their oxygen tubes as they climbed over the high terrain. It was due to Churchill's breathing problem that the altitude for the flight was kept as low as possible. They cruised at 12,000 feet between the high points and landed in Teheran, Persia (now Iran) at 8.30 a.m. on 11 August, where they were met by the British Minister in Teheran, Sir Reader Bullard. Churchill was obliged to lunch with the Shah in a palace with some spectacular views across the mountains.

Every advantage was taken on this journey. In the afternoon, in the garden of the British legation, a long conference took place with Averell Harriman and some British and American railway authorities. This meeting concerned the extended railway the allies had developed for transporting supplies to Russia. It was suggested that American personnel should now run the whole Trans-Persian rail link which had recently been completed by a British company. This had involved some highly skilful feats of engineering in an amazingly short space of time. The Americans would now supply more locomotives, rolling stock and military units specialising in working up the overall link to full capacity.

At 6.30 a.m. the following morning, 12 August the flight took off for the final leg to Moscow. Two Russian officers had now joined Churchill's plane. As the flight proceeded, one of the aircraft carrying General Wavell and others had to turn back to Teheran with engine trouble.

The Russians gave cover for the arrival of Allied aircraft entering their airspace. Great care was taken to avoid flying over battle areas, although they came close at several points. An intermediate stop was avoided to save time, and Churchill's aircraft flew on to Moscow, with all anti-aircraft batteries warned, and landed safely.

A reception full of pomp had been laid on. M Molotov, Russian generals and the entire diplomatic corps plus many photographers and reporters, awaited Churchill and Averell Harriman. Churchill pondered this strange situation — only a short time ago Stalin would have ditched the British if Hitler had behaved himself, and stuck to his treaty over the partition of Poland. Now Hitler had invaded Russian territory and the Russians had become our allies relying on British and American supplies. As Churchill had once said, 'Anyone against Hitler would have our support.' The great Russian bear and the vast frozen spaces in winter would eventually sap the strength of the Nazi regime.

Upon arrival the guard of honour was inspected by the visitors and the three national anthems were played. Together with Molotov, Winston Churchill and Averell Harriman all made short speeches into the microphone. Thence Churchill was driven to the luxurious State Villa No. 7 and Harriman stayed at the

American Embassy. An impeccable and courteous Russian officer was assigned to Churchill as his aide-de-camp.

After both visitors had settled in they dined in splendid style, but as time was short they could not dwell on this for long. Churchill had requested a meeting with Joseph Stalin that night in Moscow. Molotov suggested a time of seven o'clock.

The meeting took place in the Kremlin, and this was the first time Churchill had met the powerful Communist leader. The meeting proceeded without General Wavell, who could have made things easier when discussing Stalin's favourite topic of a second front, meaning the invasion of the French mainland across the Channel. The overall discussions lasted almost four hours. Stalin was not at all happy with the allies for not having mounted an invasion across the French north coast so far in 1942. He kept reverting to this subject and suggested on more than one occasion that the British and the Americans were afraid of fighting the Germans on land, unlike the Russian armies.

Churchill explained that we could not be ready for a full invasion until later in 1943 when one million American troops were scheduled to arrive in the UK in the spring, making twenty-seven divisions. The British would have ready a further twenty-one divisions. Almost half of the overall forty-eight divisions would be armoured. If Wavell had been present at this first meeting the military explanation would have been forcibly clear. Stalin made many adverse comments about waiting until 1943, and repeatedly said that the Russians had different attitudes about fighting the Germans etc. He became very despondent.

References were then made about our heavy bombing of the German mainland. At last Stalin agreed this was very important as it struck at the morale of the German population. However, he continually harked back about opening a second front in Europe in 1942, and inferred that the Allies were letting the Russians down in this respect. In fact no hard promises had been made for 1942 and it was explained that the British and Americans needed to work towards 1943 for this venture and make proper preparations which would have more chance of success.

Then Churchill sprang his ace card, which he had already cleared with President Roosevelt. He told Stalin in so many words that we already had a joint US British plan named 'Torch' being prepared, which must be kept strictly secret, to invade the Vichy North African coastal regions, this being the soft belly of the Nazi crocodile, with a supporting Churchillian cartoon sketched as he talked. At this point a transformation took place. Stalin grinned. He liked it and immediately grasped the tactical value of such an operation. He even made a joke about keeping it a secret from the British press, and finally said 'May God prosper this undertaking.'

It was made clear that the Allies wanted to take the strain off the Russians, but at this point we had insufficient forces and landing craft available to attack and invade effectively the northern French coast, which had been so heavily fortified. A smaller British attack in 1942, as Stalin had suggested, would have wasted manpower to no advantage.

Eventually Cadogan, Brooke, Wavell and Tedder arrived by a Russian aircraft after engine trouble in their earlier aircraft, and more meetings and discussions were planned. Churchill had been firmly polite with Stalin, who had asked for the whole Allied group to stay a little longer, but Churchill had replied that he would, but only if constructive issues could be settled – or words to that effect. It appeared that eventually a thaw set in, after some disagreeable comments by Stalin. Meetings with Russian generals were arranged and many topics discussed. Churchill was then invited to Stalin's private apartment in the Kremlin, where Stalin's red-headed daughter was shyly introduced and kissed her father. Churchill commented later that she was a nice girl, but was not allowed to stay for the refreshments and close conversation that continued, with Molotov present. They sat at table eating and drinking far too long, from 8.30 p.m. to 2.30 a.m., but now all was out in the open; a much more friendly relationship was established.

Churchill and his colleagues were due to make an early start at dawn, and both sides were content and looked forward to the overthrow of the Nazi regime. It was finally concluded that a closer friendship between the Soviet Union, Great Britain and the United States of America had been established. Stalin looked forward to further discussions as our plans unfolded. A draft of the proceedings which had taken place was prepared by Sir Alexander Cadogan. After consultation with Mr Churchill the official communiqué was issued. The return flight back to Cairo became airborne at 5.30 a.m. on 16 August and landed at Teheran for refuelling and a brief stay. Reports via the British Legation were issued, and before leaving Churchill sent his warm thanks to Stalin for his hospitality.

Upon arrival in Cairo on 17 August, a congratulatory message from King George VI awaited Churchill regarding the success of the visit, which had cleared the overall situation with the Russians. The open relationship with Stalin which had been established was considered to be of immense importance towards the eventual defeat of the Nazis. Two days later a message from General Smuts confirmed how delighted he was to have the Russians falling in with the Allies, at least as far as the progress of the war was concerned. Smuts, a great and close friend of Churchill, was so grateful and appreciative of the effort, but also understood how much strain on his health these visits were taking and implored Churchill to be careful.

Overlapping above events – 9 August

THE DEFENCE OF MALTA

In the preceding week a huge attempt to save Malta had also been underway. The enemy was desperate to overrun our strategic island fortress in the middle of the Mediterranean, having made an earlier attempt to strangle supplies. We were determined to hold on at all costs and replenish vital supplies, now almost exhausted. Operation 'Pedestal' was underway. A large convoy of fourteen fast merchant ships, one being a US tanker, had set sail with a huge protective escort of two battleships, three aircraft carriers, seven cruisers, and thirty-two destroyers.

Over the days which followed and up to 15 August, a life and death voyage took place which lost and damaged a number of our valuable ships. These included the aircraft carrier *Eagle* which was sunk, and the carrier *Indomitable*, badly damaged. Two cruisers were sunk and two more were badly damaged. A destroyer was sunk and eleven of the merchant ships were either sunk or badly damaged.

A number of aircraft from the carriers afloat had already become airborne and reached the airfield in Malta. The two battleships *Nelson* and *Rodney* left the convoy by prior arrangement before reaching the narrows where they would have become sitting ducks. It was the concentrated attack by U-boats and E-boats at night which had taken such a heavy toll on our convoy. Eventually just three undamaged merchantmen with their cargo entered the safety of the Grand Harbour in Malta. Some time later one more ship with cargo limped into port, and finally the valuable US tanker *Ohio* was towed in miraculously, with her cargo intact. Amazingly, five shiploads were sufficient to save the situation. Thirty-nine enemy aircraft had been shot down during the attack and an Italian U-boat had been destroyed.

Very soon British submarines were once again operating from Malta and a full compliment of RAF aircraft were again commanding the central Mediterranean.

During the course of the enemy attack a disagreement arose between Hitler and the Italians. The Germans wanted to use the Luftwaffe exclusively in the last stages of the action, and the Italians wished to cooperate with their navy. Hitler was not keen on the Italian naval cooperation and eventually Mussolini backed down and the Italian cruisers were withdrawn. But as they moved closer to their home port, two were torpedoed by British submarines and sank. A German officer later described the whole operation as a useless waste of fighting power. Despite the British losses it was a failure of the Axis, and the impact of this would be felt later.

19 August – At last Winston Churchill and General Montgomery were able to meet and confer in the general's desert-front caravan. General Alexander, now overall commander of HM Forces in the Middle East, had taken Churchill on a conducted tour of the desert region by car. Having arrived at Montgomery's headquarters, much was discussed and Churchill was full of praise and understanding of the plan now starting to unfold. It became clear that the change of command was achieving the desired result.

The Western Desert Air Force, and other groups such as the a hundred US mixed aircraft, made up of fighters and bombers, in the area, attacked the enemy and their supply routes across the Mediterranean and the desert. Overall a force of some 1,300 allied aircraft became available to harry Rommel still further.

The command was now decisive and the troops became happier. Much preparation had been done to align our desert armies after training and to assemble armoured divisions according to Montgomery's requirements. There was excellent cooperation between Air Marshal Tedder, Air Marshal Coningham and the Commander-in-Chief, General Alexander. Montgomery, now directing the Eighth Army, at one point cleverly outmanoeuvred Rommel's armoured column by laying a false trail. A map was left lying in the path of some German units, which depicted a safe and sound route for heavy tanks and transport. They found the map and gobbled up this disinformation, which caused the German attacking column to founder on unsafe terrain.

Many desert actions reinforced our position as the encounters progressed. It would take Montgomery six weeks to get the Eighth Army ready for an all-out offensive and to outsmart Rommel at his own game.

'Monty', as he became known, was teetotal and drank lemonade in the desert to quench his thirst. A simple sandwich alone was sufficient for him, but his mind worked overtime. He became close to his soldiers by direct contact, and his commanders under him were left in no doubt what had to be done.

The Eighth Army was now stronger than at any point hitherto. The 51st and 44th Divisions had recently arrived from the UK, and had become desert-trained. Our strength in armour had been increased to seven brigades and in excess of 1,000 tanks; around 500 of these were American-manufactured Grants and Shermans. It was said that this gave us twice as many tanks as Rommel's army, and at last for many units parity of performance. For the first time we also had highly trained artillery units operating in the Western Desert.

In September it was reckoned that the enemy had lost thirty per cent of its shipping through RAF action, and by October this rose to forty per cent. The Battle of El Alamein commenced on 23

October 1942 at 20.00 hours London time, with a full moon and bright night sky. 'Monty' had a force of three armoured divisions and the equivalent of seven infantry divisions. In order to make the most of this large formation, the movement of troops and equipment was well camouflaged, and a dummy army camp was created with dummy railway to deceive the enemy about the direction of the planned advance. Montgomery was a past master of careful preparation. Nearly 1,000 artillery pieces opened up, including the one hundred 105-millimetre self-propelled guns supplied by President Roosevelt's emergency aid.

The excellence of the British gunnery was feared by the enemy and had not been used to effect in the desert before. First the enemy batteries were bombarded for twenty minutes, and then the enemy infantry received similar attention. On top of this, the Desert Air Force bombed certain areas, which must have shaken the enemy considerably. Nevertheless, although the Germans had been taken by surprise they had prepared strong fortifications and minefields.

After the initial heavy fire of our artillery and the bombing by Allied aircraft, four divisions of British infantry pressed on to open up a two-pronged drive through the enemy's fortifications, clearing mines, closely followed by two armoured divisions.

All through the ensuing desert battle the enemy resisted strongly. First our forces would move forward, then they would be stopped by minefields and stiff resistance of enemy fire, and our armour would be hit by well tried and tested German anti-tank guns.

In the meantime, it was not known that Rommel was away from the action in a hospital in Germany. His place had been taken by a certain General Stumme. Within twenty-four hours of the British bombardment General Stumme died of a heart attack. Records show that Hitler stepped in and asked Rommel to immediately leave hospital and get back to resuming his command. Heavy fighting continued and towards the end of October the enemy air forces, both German and Italian, made a strong bid to gain superiority. There were losses on both sides, but they failed in their mission. Combat descriptions emerged and often the Italian fighter pilots would make extravagant manoeuvres, flying towards their target rolling over or flying upside down in an effort to impress. This, however, frequently resulted in them being shot down.

At one stage the enemy, both German and Italian, attempted a counter-attack following their well tried tactics, but this failed because the British armour stayed put and let the enemy tanks do the work. It appeared that they were picked off by the RAF, using eighty tons of bombs in two and a half hours of sorties, with devastating results. What a difference an air attack can make when finely tuned! Congratulatory messages from Winston Churchill were sent to the British Commanders upon their movement towards success.

The top secret 'Torch' campaign would at this point not be far away and both these actions, if successful, would produce a turning point of immense importance in the overall conflict. The desert battle had yet to be won, with the infantry continuously having to fight their way through the enemy minefields. Much fighting ensued with armour on both sides being the ultimate key to victory. Finally, Montgomery's master plan, 'Supercharge', was ready to be put into action after some clever deployment, with various units and divisions joined up to make a strong reserve. The breakthrough was to be led by the 2nd New Zealand Division, the 151st and 152nd British Infantry Brigades, and the 9th British Armoured Brigade.

On the night of 28 October and then again on the 30th the Australians attacked northwards towards the coast and finally succeeded in isolating the four German battalions remaining. This completely threw the enemy, who rapidly moved around their main forces in the vicinity to save the boxed in German battalions. The resulting fighting became intense and tied up the enemy's remaining strength, all due to the impressive advance of the Australians. Whilst this was taking place Monty was free to re-form our main forces. Thus the battle became the road to victory.

On 2 November at 1 a.m. 'Supercharge' began in earnest. A barrage of 300 guns produced an opening for the British brigades attached to the New Zealand Division to break through the enemy-defended zone. The 9th British Armoured Brigade then drove ahead according to plan. Alas! War is never straightforward

– this latest thrust forward brought our armour into another enemy defence line, which was well covered with mines and the efficient German anti-tank guns. In a long engagement the brigade suffered badly, but the path behind them remained open. Through this the 1st British Armoured Division moved forward and the last tank battle had begun. All the available enemy tanks attacked our column on each flank, but this did them no good.

Reports followed from some Allied aircraft stating that the enemy had started to retreat. However, at one strategic point known as the Rahman track the enemy rearguard action held off our main body of armour. Hitler had issued an order insisting that there must be no retreat. The German armour had tried every manoeuvre but all attacks had been repulsed. The RAF had given strong support to our forces throughout and had also attacked the retreating enemy columns. At last only one more hole had to be punched through the enemy positions. This came early on 4 November. The 5th Indian Brigade made a sudden and decisive attack on the enemy position, which was completely successful. The battle for Egypt was won at last and the Eighth Army was in position for our armour to pursue and attack the rear of the enemy in open ground. Additionally, the Desert Air Force was in pursuit of German and Italian units desperate to get away. What enemy units remained in their defensive positions were gradually cut off and eventually surrounded. Churchill, of course, gave his usual historic observations and commented that the Battle of Alamein was the turning of the 'hinge of fate' and followed this with his words 'Before Alamein we never had a victory. After Alamein we never had a defeat.'

As the battle of the desert was nearing conclusion the 'Torch' operation had at last been launched, directed at the north-west African coastal regions. Complete secrecy was essential for maximum overall success.

It had been agreed that it was preferable for the first wave of the invasion to be an all-American operation. The feeling was that American troops would get a more peaceable reception along the Vichy-held coastal regions than the British. It was also suggested that some French generals and high-ranking officers might well come over smoothly to the Allied cause and assist, thus limiting the number of casualties. If a peaceful arrival was possible so much for the good, but if Vichy wanted to fight in order to prevent German interference they would be confronted by a huge Allied Amarda.

The overall 'Torch' convoys amounted to some 650 ships. The first ships sailed from the Clyde on 22 October and by the 26th all troopships had set course, including some large American forces sailing directly from the USA towards Casablanca. The latter had been planned carefully, but there was concern about meeting the planned arrival date due to weather conditions. The US General Eisenhower was in command of this first major action combining both American and British forces, and his initial command-post was in Gibraltar. By now a new large broad runway had been developed on the Rock which stretched out into Gibraltar Bay. This was tremendously important at the time, as a considerable number of aircraft were assembled for the 'Torch' zero hour. Fourteen squadrons of fighters and others were on standby ready for operations.

Churchill and Eisenhower had already agreed that the French General Giraud would possibly be the right man to help in the peaceful entry of the US forces into the Vichy North African territories rather than de Gaulle. President Roosevelt was not happy with de Gaulle because he had played the wrong cards previously when extolling himself prior to the Dakar fiasco, which developed into a free-for-all battle with the Vichy forces. However, it was necessary to produce a sweetener for de Gaulle, as he was leader of the Free French movement based in the United Kingdom. In the passage of time, this ultimately would be the governance of Madagascar.

It was amazing that the German command had not taken any serious action against the large movements of allied shipping at this time. It appeared that their thoughts were in other directions. However, a number ships in a large convoy bound for Sierra Leone were attacked by U-boats which sank thirteen vessels, but they failed to locate the large convoys arriving from the Clyde for the 'Torch' operation, and others arriving directly from America, Later they realised an Allied operation was underway, but got the location completely wrong.

At the beginning of November it was time for President Roosevelt to present his manifesto. His first draft was sent to Churchill for his observations. This was due to be sent eventually to Marshal Pétain, as the accepted leader of so-called neutral Vichy France, to win him over to the Allied cause. Upon reading this through, Churchill immediately picked up the President's reference to Pétain as 'My dear old friend' and references to World War I. After Pétain's performance to date, Churchill felt these remarks were too kind. Without the slightest hesitation Roosevelt accepted this guidance and toned things down... it just went to show how high in his estimation Churchill was rated.

On 7 November 1942 General Giraud finally arrived in Gibraltar, having travelled from the Riviera with his two sons, and then boarded a secret British submarine captained by an American. General Eisenhower had planned this voyage to a successful conclusion. The French general believed that he would be given the command of the entire Allied forces in North Africa. He had no idea of the size of the forces operating and the plans of the overall campaign. He also did not appreciate the problems of overcoming Vichy and the German influence. It took General Eisenhower forty-eight hours to straighten him out.

The French Admiral Darlan, darling of the French Navy, was high in command, but his duties were tied to Marshal Pétain and Vichy. He played his cards close to his chest. He disliked the British and had certainly been aware of Vichy forces firing on and bombing the Allies on more than one occasion. He also had attempted to cooperate with the Germans by agreeing the passage of supplies through Vichy North African neutral territory to aid Rommel, but this had been stopped by General Weygand, who secretly wished to support the Allies. Somehow Darlan's actions appeared to be a sop to Hitler, so that neutral Vichy could maintain a limited freedom from German oppression.

Eventually the Allied 'Torch' forces headed for Algiers and the coastal regions immediately to the east and west of the port. The political US representative in north-west Africa was Robert Murphy, and he resided in Algiers. It so happened that Darlan had arrived in Algiers because of his son's serious illness. If it had not been for this factor, Darlan would have been elsewhere.

Already certain trusted French generals had been advised that 'Torch' was planned, but they had not been told that it was just hours away. General Juin was one of these and was very close to Mr Murphy. When Murphy advised Juin that an American landing was imminent, the latter was flabbergasted. He advised Murphy to tell Darlan immediately, as the French Admiral held so much authority in Vichy France, and was already in Algiers. The upshot was that Darlan became furious and thought the British were quite mad, and that now the Americans had also lost their marbles. The official French armed military police then put under arrest General Juin, Murphy and another American named Kenneth Pender, after a number of young armed pro-Allied Frenchmen had tried to rally around the general and the Americans.

Early around 2 a.m. on 8 November American and British troop landings were made in the region of Algiers, in specified locations. Most landings were successful, but due to some adverse weather the American landings took some time to be established; by morning however, these were well in place. The Royal Navy, British shipping and the RAF supported these initial landings. Darlan was unsure of where he stood but decided that he must tell Pétain that Algiers was under attack by the Americans and was about to fall.

There was some heavy resistance from official Vichy French forces directly in the centre of Algiers, and heavy shore batteries fired into two British destroyers landing American rangers. This was at first a serious initial setback, not exactly what had been expected. One destroyer was heavily damaged, and the second landed her troops but later was badly hit and sank as she was withdrawing. Many of the troops in this centre region were trapped ashore and had to surrender.

Eventually, the overwhelming US and British landings closed in and Algiers fell to American troops. By 5 p.m., a change of tune – Admiral Darlan advised Marshal Pétain that he had authorised General Juin to negotiate a surrender of the city only. From this point on Darlan was under American control, and General Juin resumed his duties under Allied direction. Surrender of Algiers then took effect from 7 p.m. Now followed much confusion, with mixed French reaction. Darlan's problem was he expected German troops would move into Vichy French territory and their flimsy protective neutrality would be lost.

Around the same time, the attack on the port of Oran and surrounding area was mounted by the US 'Centre Task Force', trained in Britain and supported by the Royal Navy. The expected strong resistance from several experienced French units did not materialise and the American landings went ahead as planned. However, a battalion of US parachute troops sent to take control of the airfields at the rear of Oran failed initially because of bad weather conditions over Spain. The aircraft became scattered and missed their dropping zone. Eventually, the airborne troops struggled on after landing and joined their comrades already ashore and eventually captured the airfield, somewhat later than planned.

Disaster struck when two ex-American coastguard cutters transferred to the Royal Navy under Lend-Lease were hit by heavy fire from coastal batteries at close range when entering the harbour after the main landings. This was an attempt to seize control of the port facilities and to prevent sabotage. Both ships were destroyed, together with the loss of almost all on board. This dangerous operation was led by Captain F T Peters RN, who miraculously survived the sinking but later was killed in an aircraft disaster when returning to the UK. He was posthumously awarded the Victoria Cross and the American DSC.

At first light French destroyers and submarines were operating in Oran Bay, but were eventually mopped up by the heavier Allied naval forces. However, the French coastal batteries continued to fire on the landings. In reply British Naval forces and aircraft bombed and bombarded heavily, with the battleship *Rodney* joining in effectively. Fighting continued for a short period and ceased on the morning of 10 November, when American forces ashore launched their final attack on the city and the French capitulated by noon.

At this point German reactions came to the fore, and a swarm of U-boats sank three large ships returning empty after the Allied landings. These attacks were not allowed to last for long. Allied reactions were swift and by the end of the month nine U-boats had been destroyed in the surrounding waters.

The French General Bethouart, the divisional commander at Casablanca, was no friend of the Germans and had been brought into the picture at a late stage. He had agreed to accept the Allies' choice of General Giraud as the Supreme French Commander from this point on, but alas Allied views, Vichy French views and Free French views did not make a good mix. It was unfortunate that Resident-General Noguès, who was against everything that did not support Vichy France, had listened to telephone conversations on his secret line and immediately alerted all possible resistance to the British and American operation. In the meantime, although the anti-German Bethouart was eager to fall in with the Allies, he did not wish to arrest his immediate chief Noguès as was required. General Noguès then used his senior position to issue orders to Vichy commanders in key positions to resist the Allies. He then arrested General Bethouart and had him tried by court martial for his support of the Allies. Bethouart had to wait for his release until the Allies overhauled the situation sometime later.

The powerful US Western Task Force which had sailed directly from America had met bad weather. Snap decisions had to be made by the US Admiral Hewitt who was in command. Fortunately his decision to proceed with the original plan was the correct one, and the weather relaxed sufficiently to allow arrival of the fleet close to the Moroccan coast before dawn on 8 November.

Three separate landings were made by the US forces in the immediate area of Casablanca. A Vichy French flotilla supported by the cruiser *Primauguet* had already been alerted by General Noguès and put to sea, meeting the whole strength of the US fleet. At the end of the engagement seven French ships and three submarines had been destroyed, suffering 1,000 casualties. Captain Mercier of the *Primauguet* died on the bridge obeying his orders, doing his duty as a French naval captain, but secretly wishing for an Allied victory over the Germans. How distressing and confused life can become in time of war!

In port at Casablanca the new, unfinished battleship *Jean Bart* lay moored and unable to sail, but with her active 15-inch guns fired on the US battleship *Massachusetts*. The US ship returned fire, resulting in the *Jean Bart* becoming a beached, burned-out wreck. By 9 November, American landings successfully moved inland. Admiral Darlan, now under the tight supervision of the American forces, had by now decided where his bread was buttered, and used his senior Vichy authority on the morning of 11 November to order Noguès to surrender. The latter admitted that after three days of fighting under his command they had lost all their fighting ships and aircraft. General Eisenhower in Gibraltar now had a political problem concerning the best leader to bring the Vichy forces over to the Allies. It was obvious that Giraud's reception had been somewhat frosty amongst the higher French echelon. Admiral Darlan on the other hand appeared to get instant support from high-ranking Vichy officers. He was also high in command to the ageing Marshal Main, and had been responsible for building a strong French Navy twice over. He was highly respected by his fellow senior commanders in Vichy France and had a strong character. Unfortunately he hated the British but at last realised the truth about the necessity of stopping the Germans.

Underlying the problem presented to Eisenhower was another situation. Laval, a sly and troublesome senior Vichy minister, was playing his own power game. He had already been summoned to see Hitler in Berchtesgaden, representing Marshal Main, but had been delayed by fog. He did not arrive for the meeting until the late afternoon of 10 November, when Hitler embarked on a Franco-German history lesson. Laval was then given a joint German-Italian written demand for French consent to allow Axis landings in Tunisia. The following morning Laval was awakened with a fait accompli and told that the Führer had ordered the German Army to occupy the free Vichy zone of France. On the same day the Italians occupied Nice and Corsica. Overall this amounted to the end of Vichy as a neutral state.

Enter American General Mark Clark, acting as General Eisenhower's deputy in the field, who quickly summed up the overall situation so far as he saw it, without the knowledge of Laval's visit to Hitler. Negotiations had been proceeding in Algiers with Admiral Darlan and other French leaders, some already in France with Marshal Pétain. There were many, both British and Americans, who were aghast that the Allies were dealing with a French Admiral who had previously supported and even helped German forces to wage war against the common cause. French nationals had died fighting and killing the very people who had come to release them from the Nazi yoke and give them back their country. The Vichy government had produced a strange form of patriotism.

In the meantime General Giraud had not been accepted by the high-ranking French officers, but was prepared to work with Darlan to bring things round to the Allied cause, particularly when he heard of the occupation of German troops on Vichy French territory.

Then an emissary of General de Gaulle, General François d'Astier de la Vigerie, arrived on an unofficial visit to Algiers to assess the feeling towards his chief and to officially offer Free French forces to Giraud and to General Eisenhower – yet another complication. It appeared that the Free French and a monarchist element were separately opposed to Darlan.

Suddenly, in the afternoon of 24 December, Darlan drove from his villa to his office in Algiers and on reaching the entrance door was shot by a young man, Bonnier de la Chapelle. Darlan died on the operating table close by within one hour. The twenty-year-old killer had thought himself to be a saviour of France from evil leadership. He was tried by court martial under orders from Giraud and executed dramatically by firing squad.

The murder of Admiral Darlan had created a wholly new situation. General Giraud was the French leader originally chosen by the Allies, and now had been elected high commissioner and commander-in-chief by a leading group of French nationals. Eisenhower arrived on the scene and made it clear that Giraud would be accepted as the French leader by the Allies.

De Gaulle was hot on the trail of developments and started to promote his views to Giraud. Churchill was keeping a close eye on the Free French. De Gaulle had already told Giraud they should meet on French soil, in either Algeria or Chad, both being African French territories available at that time. Already some 100,000 Free French soldiers had joined the Allied forces. These were mainly trained native troops, in need of better equipment and organisation.

Meanwhile, strong German forces had started to arrive by air in Tunis and were getting prepared to resist the Allied advance eastwards. More enemy forces followed by sea. Limited numbers of German aircraft started to appear, and had the advantage of operating from established airfields rather than the temporary airstrips being used by the Allies as they advanced. By December on the north African coast the rainy season had begun. Our airstrips became waterlogged and gradually the advance slowed. Eventually the German aircraft, though small in numbers, were able to operate more effectively from their established airfields and a German counter-attack developed. On 22 December the Allies renewed a limited advance, but conditions were so bad that by Christmas Eve General Eisenhower decided to put the overall advance on hold. The plan was to fortify the Allied position, protect the airstrips held and await better weather conditions before proceeding further.

As the year 1942 drew to a close, Montgomery and the Eighth Army advancing westward along the North African coast had covered 1,200 miles and squeezed Rommel's forces to virtual destruction. By Christmas Day Sirte in Tripolitania had been occupied, together with some useful airfields.

The 'Torch' campaign, gradually and painfully, was producing a successful result. The Allies now needed to plan ahead carefully, and a joint meeting became necessary. Ultimately a conference in Casablanca was planned. The location suited President Roosevelt, despite his disabled condition, and also he wished to travel in secrecy to avoid public disapproval. Joseph Stalin really wished to join the conference but could not leave his soldiers during the bitter fighting in hand. He trusted Winston Churchill to keep him informed of progress. General de Gaulle was also invited but became very haughty, as he did not accept the Allies' choice of General Giraud as the French commander. Initially he refused to come, but eventually Churchill informed him via the Foreign Secretary that unless he joined the conference the Allies would, in so many words, make decisions without him, which could be far-reaching. This did the trick he finally but grudgingly agreed to come.

On 12 January, Churchill and Marshal of the RAF, Sir Charles Portal, were on course for Casablanca, flying in the Commando aircraft at a height of 8,000 feet over the Atlantic, when Churchill – having a well deserved doze in his bunk – felt his foot (close to a heating outlet) getting extremely hot. Other outlet points were also found to be burning hot. Then Churchill with another passenger explored this further. They found the heater in the converted bomb alley was being operated by two crew men using petrol inside the cabin. With the petrol vapour and heater in use they became alarmed, and for safety had this turned off. They decided that freezing was preferable to being burned alive.

(This is no exaggeration – months later, I too personally experienced the use of a similar heating unit in an American-built Vultee Vengeance, which I flew myself. At altitude, we never risked using this component for the same reason.)

In due course the main players for the Casablanca conference arrived with their supporting staff, and all found the arrangements made were superb. The hotel had surround villas marked out for the VIPs – Churchill, Roosevelt, Giraud and de Gaulle (if he should arrive). The top military commanders and staff stayed in the hotel complex.

A full conference of the Combined Chiefs of Staff was called by President Roosevelt and Winston Churchill on 20 January, 1943. They discussed the way ahead. General Alexander, at the time, was proposed by Churchill to become the Deputy Commander-in-Chief to Eisenhower. The US General Marshall asked to record formally the outstanding contribution and skill Admiral Cunningham had afforded to the Allied forces in North Africa. President Roosevelt paid tribute to Field Marshal Sir John Dill for his indispensable link between the United States and British Chiefs of Staff on military policy. Additionally, we had the executive command of the navy under Admiral Cunningham and the air force under Air Marshal Tedder.

The taste of victory, though early as yet, was not denied, but a lot more fighting and planning had to be accomplished before Germany and Japan were truly in the bag. The relations between Eisenhower and Alexander could not be better, with Eisenhower trusting Alexander with the entire direction of the battle ahead.

Eventually, de Gaulle arrived on 22 January, and immediately became difficult. At first he would not contact General Giraud in the next villa. Eventually, Churchill talked to de Gaulle and informed him that unless he cooperated, the Allies would have to break with him. Ultimately, common sense prevailed and the two Frenchmen met each other and talked for several hours and the ice was broken. De Gaulle then met President Roosevelt and surprisingly they got on well together.

Churchill had several difficult meetings with de Gaulle, but somehow made allowances for his arrogance, feeling the spirit of France flowing from his personality – although at that time he was an exile under sentence of death by the French Vichy leaders, he now relied upon the British Government and the United States.

Finally, on the 24th, all the meetings came to an end. At the press conference which followed, Churchill and Roosevelt arranged the seating so that Giraud and de Gaulle sat alternately between them, and in public made them shake hands before the reporters and cameras, which got a laugh later when the daily papers appeared.

Before Roosevelt returned home, Churchill, with boyish enthusiasm, arranged to take him to see Marrakech and to see the sun setting on the snows of the Atlas Mountains. This entailed a long drive across the desert accompanied by their immediate staff, with military escorts and aircraft patrolling overhead. There was, no doubt, a truly powerful bond between the two great leaders of the free world.

Before Churchill returned home, he took an exhausting tour, in the Commando aircraft, of the various key areas around the Mediterranean, which had been discussed at Casablanca. This included the possibility of building up the Turkish armed forces, and to supply better aircraft which could be used strategically to add to the German squeeze at the time of successful Russian advances. There was still so much to be achieved in all theatres, but the Allies were firmly set on course towards their final goal.

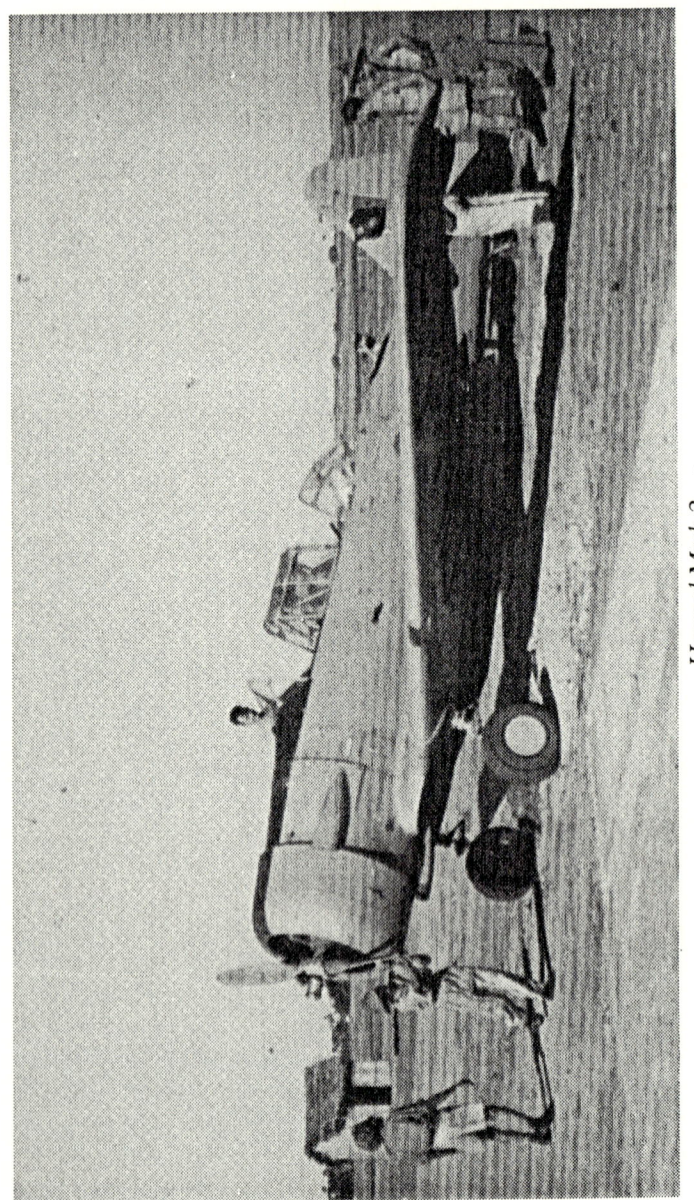

Harvard Mark 2

Chapter Ten
A MOVEMENT TO INDIA

Our group, en route for our posting to India, boarded a train in Bulawayo and retraced our journey back to Durban, arriving on 23 September 1943. Just before leaving we heard unofficially that we would learn to fly an aircraft unknown to us, and our thoughts revolved around this future experience.

Whilst awaiting our ship to take us to India, we were booked into the Clairwood Transit Camp. Together with a number of comrades from our posting, with nothing much to do, we decided to take a look at the main township. This involved a short train journey on a local line. The carriages were not unlike the London District Line trains. A young coloured pilot, well educated and said to have a princely African background, was at a loose end and decided to come along with us. He had not been on our flying course and had been passed through Clairwood from some other point in Africa.

We entered at one end of a partially empty carriage and sat together in a group. Suddenly, after a stop, the effect of apartheid suddenly became apparent. The guttural voice of a true Boer further down the compartment was raised up, telling us to throw out our coloured pilot. We told our friend to take no notice. The voice got louder and louder and more insulting. Fortunately our stop came up, and we all trooped off the train with our friend from the flying fraternity in the middle of our small group. If the journey had been any longer things could have developed into something quite nasty. It was an ignorant mistake of someone in the RAF to route our coloured companion through a South African transit camp!

In due course our ship, the HMT *Indrapoera*, arrived in dock to take us on our posting to India. We embarked on 17 October 1943, and the voyage was not so long as our previous experience. The air temperature was warm and comfortable cruising across the Indian Ocean and Arabian Sea, and it felt somehow safer, with less chance of U-boat attacks in these waters.

The most notable feature of this voyage was the large number of native African troops who filled the lower deck, and I would say they had not long been in the pay of the British army. Many bore their tribal markings on their faces, and the deep rumbling of their African voices was evident when passing by their sections. They were no trouble and we understood they would mainly become carriers of equipment for the 14th Army in Burma.

Eventually the broad landfall of the Indian subcontinent came into view, and as we drew closer the strange, faintly sweet smell of burning cow-dung mixed with other unknown substances drifted towards us in the warm air, giving a touch of mystery, a totally different atmosphere to the Africa we had left behind. We disembarked in Bombay on 5 November 1943. We stayed close to the reception centre in Worli Bombay, awaiting our travel arrangements which would take us far north to Peshawar on the NW Frontier. We passed the time largely in conversation about our surroundings and by looking at the hawk-like birds which dived and swooped continuously, looking for scraps of food, and were given a name in RAF parlance which described them perfectly, but was not their true ornithological title!

Shortly, our travel arrangements came through and our first experience of Indian rail travel was upon us, on 8 November. Some time after we left Bombay behind, the scenery slowly developed into a few clusters of palm and similar tropical growth, and here and there small dilapidated homes with very little happening came into view. The odd sleepy Indian bullock, continuously chewing away at nothing much in the way of fodder, and the occasional paddy field here and there, completed the vista. From time to time we stopped at small stations, where *char wallahs* with their tea-making contraptions plied their trade, together with others selling fruit etc., which one had to be careful of eating in case of contact with contaminated water.

The overall journey became somewhat tortuous as there did not seem to be a direct rail link in certain areas. We slept here and there, and fed at planned stops. There was some shunting and changes of direction as we linked up to the main sections of the rail track. Gradually the landscape became more rugged in appearance as we approached our destination.

Finally, on 11 November, we reached the end of our journey after some 1,350 miles, and the noise of the aircraft flying overhead was confirmation enough. Upon looking into the sky the rather large single-engined aircraft gave us our first view of the Vultee Vengeance which we would eventually fly.

The 152 Operational Training Unit in Peshawar was originally an old army cantonment and the building in which we initially stayed had the background and appearance of something out of a Rudyard Kipling story. The RAF had taken over the whole cantonment and built a long permanent runway stretching out towards the inhospitable terrain.

(Some years later when talking to my future father-in-law, I discovered that in 1919 after World War I when in the Royal Horse Artillery, he had been posted to the very same cantonment. When on horseback escorting a team of camels taking supplies up to the troops on the frontier, he nearly lost one animal when crossing Attock Bridge and had trouble extracting the unfortunate beast from its predicament. In 1943 Attock Bridge was a pinpoint for me when flying in the area. Stories of this ilk can do wonders for young men when talking to their future fathers-in-law!)

Our flying course commenced with a refresher flying Harvards. My instructor was F/O Ahmad from the background of an Indian squadron, and I found him friendly and got along with him quite well. We covered local familiarisation, circuits and landings, forced landings, runway landings, low flying, aerobatics, formation flying, diving, and instrument flying – both as safety pilot and under the hood. Then came a cross-country exercise, and one of the ground staff, an A/C Hughes, came along for a ride.

Finally it was time to sample the aircraft we had travelled half way across the world to fly: the American-built Vultee Vengeance two-seater dive bomber which was powered by a 1,700 hp Wright Cyclone double-row radial air-cooled engine.

This aircraft could dive vertically – virtually 90° to the ground. The infamous German Stuka dived at a mere 60° to 80° maximum and was not so fast or controllable. Obviously diving at 90° is more accurate for bombing. This was achieved by a zero angle of incidence of the main plane and a high fin and rudder.

Slatted dive-brakes which opened above and below each wing helped to stabilise the speed in the vertical dive and allowed the pilot to align more accurately on the target.

The second crew member, at the time called an observer (whose flying badge was an 'O' with half wing, and who was later called a navigator), performed the duties of navigator, wireless operator and rear gunner with twin Browning machine guns, and sat in the rear of the aircraft.

Also in the rear section of the aircraft was an emergency control column. This could be slotted in for control in the event of the pilot being hit by enemy fire whilst in a vertical dive, enabling the navigator to pull out and make his exit by parachute. There was also a duplicate throttle lever to control the engine speed, but only to be used in an emergency.

The precarious drill for abandoning the aircraft from both cockpits was to clamber down the footholds in the side of the fuselage and release oneself at the lowest point. This was necessary because there was every chance that one would collide with the large tail-plane and fin if one baled out straight from the cockpit. This whole escape thing was regarded by all as a joke, and the most favourable option for this aircraft was to make a wheels-up belly crash landing, if this was feasible.

Before we actually started to fly the Vengeance, we were given a health check and a session in the decompression chamber controlled by a very helpful specialist medical officer, F/Lt Walker. An entry was then made in our log books if we were cleared to fly the course. My entry reads:

> Tested in Decompression Chamber at Peshawar up to 40,400 ft.
> Remained above 30,000 ft for 15 minutes. Witnessed the effect of Anoxia at 25,000 ft. No ill effects from high altitude. No ear or sinus trouble during descent.
> Certified true statement 7.12.43. Signed K N Walker F/Lt

The first flight in the Vengeance was with my instructor. I sat in the rear section with the emergency control column slotted in for use. This was the only way to get some idea of the feel of the aircraft. My instructor took off and talked me through the various aspects of the aircraft as we flew around for thirty minutes. There were several important peculiarities to the Vengeance which made it unique. Firstly, the zero angle of incidence of the main plane enabled the 90° dive. However, this feature meant that to get the necessary lift on take-off the wing flaps had to be lowered by 15°. Even so, the aircraft still needed a long runway. To marginally overcome this, the drill for take-off was to stand on the brakes, open the throttle fully with stick held back in the stomach to keep the tail down, then, with everything quivering, release the brakes, centralise the stick and proceed with normal take-off. The undercarriage was raised up when airborne, followed by the gentle raising of the flaps as the aircraft climbed away.

Following the first flight in the rear section with my instructor, I proceeded with my first solo flight for thirty minutes and found that, apart from the unusual take-off procedure, the aircraft handled well and was not difficult to land, mainly, I thought, due to its weight.

The importance of the correct take-off procedure was suddenly brought home to us when one of our star performers, a beefy Scot who, when taking off on his first solo Vengeance flight, forgot to put down his 15° of flap. With his throttle wide open, he reached the end of the long runway with his tail lifted but was still not airborne, and careered onto rough ground. He told us later that he took his feet off the rudder pedals and braced them up in front, then pulled the stick with all his might. The tail crashed downwards, the tail wheel broke off, and he bounced into the air. He landed later without a tail wheel, a bent tail and a red face; at least he had brought the aircraft back, but he had some explaining to do!

We all proceeded with another local solo flight, practising steep turns, followed by our first dual dive and low flying. For this we sat in the back with instructor up front demonstrating the 90° dive from 10,000 feet, and the effect of the dive-brakes and pulling out at 3,000 feet.

We pilots had already paired off with our navigators who at this point were being instructed in their back seat activities – navigating, wireless operation and air gunnery. We were all mostly sergeants, not long out of training. My navigator was a friendly tall Londoner, Doug Terry.

In the meantime all pilots had now experienced a number of solo dives and low flying, and finally formation dives. A particular formation suited to dive-bombing was the box of four. If one could imagine four aircraft suddenly appearing overhead and delivering their bombs one after the other aimed at the same point it could be quite devastating. It had been said that the Japanese enemy really feared such an attack.

The box of four was in fact a 'V' formation of three aircraft with the fourth aircraft formatting beneath and slightly behind the leader. Nobody really favoured flying in the fourth position. It was the most critical in the whole formation. One had to look upwards at the aircraft above and anticipate any downward movement. In a dive-bombing exercise, the leader would give the command to echelon starboard. Number four would move upwards beside number two and number three would drop below and move up beside number four. The leader, being number one, would then position the target where the leading edge of the port wing joins the fuselage; he would open his bomb doors and then roll over into his dive, closing his cooling gills. He would not put his dive-brakes out until well into his dive. The other three aircraft would roll over with bomb doors open and cooling gills closed, following behind and spacing out with dive-brakes progressively opened. All bombs would be released as each aircraft reached 3,000 feet, pulled out with dive-brakes and bomb doors closed, with cooling gills slightly opened and then shallow dive away at low level, maintaining as much speed as possible.

Initially these formation diving exercises were done without using practice smoke-bombs, and without our navigators. On one occasion a devil-may-care vicar's son completely forgot to put out his dive-brakes and the result was – whoosh! He caught up and passed his somewhat shocked predecessor in a vertical dive. Fortunately there was no accident and we all had a nervous restricted laugh!

Eventually it was time for our navigator crew members to join in the fun, and their very first flight was in a box of four formation diving exercise. In such an exercise the man in the rear section of the aircraft had to swivel around facing the tail and comb the air for imaginary enemy fighters – this meant diving

Two-seated dive-bomber

Doug Terry and self

vertically facing backwards, which was really throwing them in at the deep end without any practice. What with this unusual and astonishing technique of a Vengeance take-off, they must have been somewhat startled, and wondered about their future!

However, the next exercise with our crew members was a cross-country flight, which was an hour and twenty minutes cruise around the N. W. Frontier. They could at last use their navigating skills, and no doubt they were happier.

The course continued with all manner of exercises, such as air-to-air combat using cine, then followed numerous dive-bombing exercises using smoke-bombs. Normally we would climb up to 10,000 feet four times in one trip, dropping one smoke bomb each time on the target range. Then followed exercises when our rear man fired his twin Browning guns at ground targets, then followed a front-wing gun exercise. Finally, formation cross- country exercises with a box of four formation dive bombing run upon return, produced complete dummy operations.

At the end of one busy week's flying, the commanding officer arranged a relaxing tour of the old native city of Peshawar for those who were interested. We were escorted around by the official *dandi wallah* Indian police. It was interesting to see the layout of the narrow streets or alleys, where each street specialised in one particular trade.

We arrived at the shoemaker's section, and I was surprised to see a stall where the curly toed tribesman's 'Ali Baba' shoes were displayed. I became interested to see the real article as often illustrated in story books, and thought a pair would make a good souvenir. I did not wish to show too much eagerness to make a purchase, as the price would then certainly increase dramatically. I gently toyed with a shoe and noted the sound craftmanship of leather combined with tough green threads and a green inner sole with coloured decoration. These shoes were no doubt intended for a tribesman's best occasional apparel. Without actually yawning, I looked at other shoes and casually asked the price of the first pair. 'Thirty rupees, sahib' said the shoemaker. I had been in India long enough to know that one never coughs up cash against the first rendering. I did my best to sound disinterested and gradually chiselled him down to twenty rupees, suddenly I looked around me and saw that I was surrounded by a group of what appeared to be a small band of fierce bearded tribesmen from the Khyber... and horror upon horror there was no sign of my group of RAF colleagues in sight! Only a short time previously I had heard the story of someone within the confines of our cantonment who had been stabbed by a tribesman.

I agreed the price quickly, put down my twenty rupees, grabbed the shoes, doing my best to look as friendly as possible to the company at large, and moved off, determined to put as much space between myself and the tribesmen without showing any sign of panic. I turned the corner, shot down the next alley and to my relief spied my party ahead.

No sooner had I reached my friends, when around the corner came the shoemaker, coming towards us waving a shoe and followed by his small band of onlookers. 'Sahib, sahib' shouted the shoemaker, 'you have two left-footed shoes and here is the right one.' There followed a quick change of one shoe with the barely different shape of the replacement, and the shoemaker and all the bearded ones were nodding and smiling, happy at a wrong being put right. It seemed that in these parts, all within earshot of a purchase are only too pleased to join in the proceedings and get to grips with the finer points of the trading.

Shortly after this interlude, one of the *dandi wallah* police decided to show us the police station or barracks. We passed an empty cell where a ball and chain lay casually on the floor, reminiscent of a medieval dungeon! Then we were told that a prisoner was being brought in – an Indian soldier on leave, who had walked into his home and stabbed an interloper he found with his wife. This was told with the casual manner of being nothing particularly unusual.

We were then escorted up to the flat roof in the open air above and treated to strong tea and a mound of brightly coloured iced cakes, protected from the teaming flies orbiting above by a fine net. This was a local speciality, and, one could say, a tribesman's delight. The technique was to lift a corner of the net, grab a cake, and then swiftly pass to the mouth before the flies descended. On the whole the lads did quite well and we thanked the chief *dandi wallah* and with much hand shaking prepared to depart. At that point the chief spied the Ali Baba shoes I was clasping under my arm, and enquired how much I had paid – I told him twenty rupees. He gave me a knowing smile and said fifteen rupees would have been ample.

The following day several of my friends and I visited an open market close to the cantonment, and in wandering around I found a pack of photographs supposedly depicting local views etc. Within the pack I found a photograph of a local tribeswoman in voluminous tribal dress, crouched in a rocky grotto with the appearance of one bent on knifing her husband. Another photograph was of a heavily moustached decapitated tribesman's head with complete ragged head cloth, propped up on rough stony ground. Just the kind of holiday snaps to send to your friends!

On studying these photographs, it seemed just as well that all our Vengeance aircraft carried a notice in several languages stating in so many words that 'A reward of 100 rupees in silver will be paid if the crew of the aircraft forced-landed is returned unharmed.'

Around this time a Vengeance crew from a previous course suddenly arrived back in Peshawar after such an adventure. Apparently the pilot had managed to make a successful forced landing, but they were promptly captured and taken to Kabul as prisoners. At the time Afghanistan was a neutral country and in Kabul there were embassies of Britain, Germany and Japan. Somehow the British Ambassador worked wonders and after a period they were returned. The full details were not released to us at the time, but the crew were unharmed and our ground crew later went into tribal territory and brought the broken aeroplane back on a transporter. We all wondered how many sacks of silver rupees had been paid out to cover such an operation.

All through history the tribes on the NW Frontier have strongly resisted strangers, but if a reward was ever offered they would fall over backwards to get it.

Christmas 1943 brought us a well-earned festive luncheon in camp which was much appreciated. The bearers distributed garlands at table, as was the custom on the frontier for such occasions, which seemed to be a strange mixture of habits for such a rugged lawless society.

The overall flying course gradually drew to a close after cramming in a number of formation cross-country flights and a further fourteen bombing dives. According to my log book I had made a total of fifty vertical dives from 10,000 feet. Most of these flights had been with my navigator Doug Terry, who also had an altimeter in the rear. According to instructions he would have announced on each dive over the intercom as we plummeted to the critical point, 'Three thousand feet.' This was a safety procedure laid down initially to make sure the pilot had sufficient height left to pull out whilst concentrating on the target.

At the end of the course we were given the final assessment, and I got the usual 'average' comment for each item – dive bomber pilot, pilot-navigator, and in bombing – but in air gunnery I got a below average comment. This I could not understand as we had only used the front guns twice. Doug had given me the number of the target and he had said I had made a good hit, certainly on one occasion. So I was a bit disappointed. However, no one ever mentioned their assessment, so possibly I was not alone, or maybe I aimed at the wrong target. In any situation, firing the front guns in the Vengeances was not a very accurate pastime, as there was no illuminated target sight on the front windshield and it amounted to looking across the cowling and hoping for the best. A bit like a coconut shy.

After all this highly tuned training we were presented with an anticlimax. The Vultee Vengeance in the meantime had suddenly become unsuitable for the Burma campaign. The ongoing war had gradually moved farther southwards as the 14th Army gradually pushed the enemy back, where airstrips were temporary and shorter in length. The Vengeance needed a long run to get off the ground, so it was rapidly being replaced by squadrons of Hurricanes, which could land and take off easily on short airstrips. As the Americans would say, the war had become a whole new ball game. However, our training to fly the somewhat unusual Vengeance was not entirely wasted, as a number of units distributed far and wide in India continued to fly them for special duties.

At once a requirement arose for a posting of three crews to join a flight of Vengeances attached to the Air Fighting Training Unit at Amarda Road. This was situated on the eastern edge of Orissa, some twenty-five miles from the coast and roughly 110 miles from Calcutta. Our second Indian train journey was now imminent and we would have to travel approximately another 1,300 miles to reach our destination.

On 17 January 1944 we gathered our kit together and the whole course assembled on the Peshawar Railway Station platform. There was quite a crowd with both pilots and navigators, various groups all starting from the same point but ultimately destined for different air stations or squadrons all over the subcontinent.

We waited and waited and started to get a bit fidgety. Suddenly the faint metallic clinking and puffing of a steam loco heralded something moving in our direction, and sure enough a train eventually slowly arrived on our platform. No sooner had it stopped than two super-energetic types shot into an empty compartment, and immediately shot out again on to the platform shouting 'Don't get in! There's s—t inside the roof against the luggage rack!' Immediately someone close to a telephone point phoned the air station and talked to Medical Officer F/Lt Walker, friend of all aircrew and guardian of the decompression chamber. He was told that the whole course had refused to get on the train and the reason. In a surprisingly short time things started to happen. The train drew out of the station. Soon after another train puffed into view and stopped on our platform. All was well, there were no further problems and our long journey commenced.

We three crews had a journey before us similar in mileage to our first Indian train journey but in a different direction. We experienced much the same problems with rail links, eating and sleeping. At one point the train stopped in the middle of nowhere, and a soldier travelling on our train decided he wanted some tea. A number of our group were stretching their legs and in the absence of any *char wallahs* we saw the soldier calmly take out his billycan, walk up to the engine-driver and ask for some hot water. Without hesitation the engine-driver pulled a lever inside the cab and a gush of steaming boiling water poured out beneath the footplate into the soldier's billycan. Virtually tea on demand. There's no doubt that British soldiers in India had been around for a long time, and these tricks of the trade have been passed down through the years.

After six days and corresponding uncomfortable nights, with planned and unplanned stops, we finally arrived at our destination on 23 January 1944.

Our arrival at the Air Fighting Training Unit, Amarda Road was low key, and our quarters were located in a long native-built hut. The outer walls were made of some thick-coated textile suited to a tropical climate, which at times could become both hot and humid. A large punka hung from the centre of the hut which a bearer would pull very occasionally during the day when the temperature became excessively hot. Our beds were the traditional Indian charpoys, together with mosquito nets.

In due course we reported to, what was broadly known as the Target Towing Flight. It appeared that the Vengeance was an ideal aircraft for towing large drogues used as targets for fighter aircraft firing practice. The rear section of the Vengeance could comfortably house the winch for paying out the drogue, which after the exercise could be dropped and collected for scrutiny. The fighter aircraft's rounds would sometimes be coloured so that the pilot firing the rounds could be identified.

Apart from this use, the Vengeance, although designed as a two-seater aircraft, had enough space in the rear section to cram in up to three passengers. This was a rough and ready way of air travel for fairly short flights in the area, up to a maximum radius of approximately 400 miles. Occasionally this would create a requirement for a navigator/wireless operator.

After just one local flight to familiarise ourselves with the immediate surroundings, with one of the ground staff joy-riding in the back seat, we had an enforced break to our activities. The Americans arrived in force for a period and more or less took over the airfield for a big airlift, using flights of Curtis Commando aircraft to fly urgent supplies over the Hump.

There was a very noticeable difference in the way the Yanks serviced their aircraft in comparison to the RAF. Our fitters and riggers made do with whatever limited components were available, and for example would almost rebuild an existing engine if necessary. The Americans, on the other hand, would take out a faulty engine and immediately replace with a completely new engine. In consequence, along the length of the Amarda Road runway a number of discarded US engines which had been taken from Commando aircraft and exchanged for completely new engines lay awaiting collection. Expense did not come into the picture.

Eventually the US airlift wound down, and we returned to our normal flying duties and commenced some flights involving drogue towing, and one in which I flew was an experimental drogue height test, with Doug Terry streaming the drogue, helped by a Sgt. Eley. Another unusual drogue flight was towed for a Wellington bomber, for the turret gunners' practice.

Flights into Calcutta came up quite regularly and landed at both Alipore and Dum Dum. Drogues for target towing were streamed by all three of our navigators, but they were not really happy unless they could use the skills for which they were trained. They were not required for the short Calcutta trips, and in reality the ground staff were quite capable of streaming the drogues. 23 May produced a flight which remains embedded in my mind. Something strange was going on behind the scenes for the use of the Vultee Vengeance. Possibly a new area of use was in the wind for this aircraft, or another battleground was opening up where the Vengeance could be used effectively. Whatever the reason, a wing commander from Delhi turned up with a specially prepared Vengeance No. 781 which had a modification to the forks in the bomb bay. This would apparently enable a better release of the bombs in the vertical dive and throw the forks more accurately to the farthest extent away from the arc of the airscrew. Already the forks worked effectively, but apparently the modification would produce more precision in the release.

It was my job to drop two 500-pound bombs located in the bomb bay of the special Vengeance in a dive from 10,000 feet, and the Wing Commander flying a Hurricane, would attempt to watch the bombs release. My two colleague pilots, Derek Killey and Bobbie Brazier, and I concluded that a Hurricane could never hold a Vengeance in a vertical dive, so why not use another Vengeance in the exercise – but who were we to cast such doubt on the exercise?

I arrived at dispersal. The Vengeance was already bombed up awaiting the action. I was advised by an armourer that the bombs would be fused when I switched on the fuse switch adjacent to the throttle quadrant, and the switch would glow red, and when I released the bombs by pressing the button on top of the throttle the red light would extinguish, indicating the bombs had gone. The bombs would be dropped in the sea three or four miles off the deserted coast. I was only able to have a quick word with the Wing Commander before the flight, and as RT communication between Vengeance and Hurricane was not available I said that I would waggle my wings before I went into the dive.

When I got into the aircraft I found I had a passenger in the rear seat who was coming along for the ride. Initially I thought he was someone with technical knowledge to observe the fun, but this was far from the truth. He had flown in with the Wing Commander and was possibly his batman.

Both aircraft took off – I led and the Hurricane followed and then pulled up on my starboard wing, well spaced out. I climbed steadily with the weight of 1,000 pounds of bombs on board and headed out towards the coast. My idea was to climb up to 10,000 feet, but I found the rate of climb was so slow I decided to make the dive from just over 9,000 feet, which was high enough, and then thought if I made a short shallow dive and then pulled up we could make a few more feet, but this made no difference at all.

We were about four miles out to sea, it was bright sunshine and not a soul in sight in whichever direction one looked. To me the whole thing seemed to be somewhat haphazard, and my passenger sat peaceably in the back. I could still see the Hurricane well spaced out on my starboard wing.

This was it – I waggled my wings, opened the bomb doors in the belly of the aircraft, I switched on the red fuse light, closed the cooling gills, closed the throttle slightly and rolled over into the dive and opened my dive brakes – 3,000 feet came up on the altimeter – I pressed the bombing button then pulled out, closing the bomb doors and dive brakes and opened the cooling gills...

absolutely nothing had happened. I asked my passenger if he saw an explosion... a rather quiet voice in the back said 'No.' There was no sign of the Hurricane... what had happened to the Wing Commander?

Then I glanced at the fuse switch and this was still glowing red. Immediately it occurred to me that we had a hang-up with two live 500-pound bombs lurking beneath us in the bomb bay. Oh boy! we must do something quick.

I told my passenger that I would open the bomb doors flying straight and level and see if I could release the bombs again, and told him to keep a sharp lookout in the sunshine and shadow of the aircraft to see if any bombs dropped in the sea.

I went through this procedure. The answer came back 'No nothing.' Just after this attempt our engine started to cough and lose power. We had already regained some height after the dive and were now flying at about 2,500 feet.

Now we were starting to lose height somewhat dramatically. Thoughts flashed across my mind, and I told my passenger to open his canopy as I opened mine... I thought quickly that I would put the aircraft down in the surf along the beach... then I asked my passenger if he knew if the fuel system had been altered – just a long shot, but he knew absolutely nothing. (Our Vengeances at Amarda Road had all fuel tanks linked together – at 152 OTU, we had a row of electric fuel pump switches). We were low and still losing height. For some unknown reason I suddenly looked downwards by my seat and there almost out of sight low down was a manual fuel selector like the Harvard. I turned the fuel cock and the engine sprang healthily back into life. Hurrah! What joy, we were back in the world in one piece... but we still had the question about the unwanted live bombs.

I decided to have another try at clearing whatever was still in the bomb bay. Again I told my new comrade-in-distress to look carefully at the shadow of the aircraft on the water again to see if anything dropped off when I waggled things around, with the bomb doors opened. Absolutely nothing dropped out. So I decided to fly back to base and try to get the watch office to take a look as I flew over before landing. Oh dear! It was not one of the best characters on duty to ask, and I recognised his voice.

I flew around and explained the predicament over the RT, and described about the red fuse light, and that I had made two attempts at trying to shake a possible hang up out of the bomb bay. 'Would they now please take a look if I flew slowly over with bomb doors open?' A rather unfeeling annoyed answer came back instantaneously, 'Take it away and try again.'

There was complete silence in the back seat, my passenger must be getting worried, and I was not feeling particularly good myself. We flew back out to sea again and repeated the process... absolutely nothing... so I returned to base and flew around the circuit again, and rather sternly I repeated the request and said that they had better do something as fuel was getting low... I thought this might create some thoughts... so I would be coming down soon, before we fell out of the sky. Begrudgingly the same voice said 'Hold on – we'll take a look.' I guess someone high up had arrived on the scene. I opened bomb doors and flew slowly directly over the watch office... 'All clear, you may land.' Oh! what a relief.

I taxied back to dispersal and parked. The Wing Commander was hovering around and the only comment he made was, 'When trying to make height, keep holding a climbing attitude' – he was referring to my short dive and pulling up at the beginning of the exercise. He made no further comment. I wondered how successful he had been in his Hurricane.

In the meantime a colleague, Derek Killey, had his ear to the ground and heard the comment that the armourers had said the bombs had only been fused in the tail, when for dropping in the sea they should have been fused both in the nose and the tail. Also someone thought that I had not fused the bombs, but when they looked in the bomb bay the telltale plates were dangling freely, which proved the bombs had been fused correctly. Nothing was said about the red fuse warning light which had stayed on. No further comments were made, so we never found out if the wing commander had been able to assess the performance of his modified forks used for releasing the bombs in a vertical dive. The Vengeance brought in for the test had been flown away so we would never have the chance to find out about the wiring up of the bombs in the test. I had the feeling that the wing commander had not managed to see much at all because a Hurricane could never hold a Vengeance in a 90° dive and he was not going to talk about that!

Somewhere three or four miles off the coast of Orissa in the Bay of Bengal, my two heavily corroded 500-pound bombs must still be lying there deeply imbedded in the silt of the sea bed!

On 31 May 1944 an American Lt McFayden (USAAF), currently involved with technical service or suchlike at Amarda Road, needed to visit an American airbase at Madaiganj. It was my turn to make the trip. I plotted the course and arrived on the Madaiganj circuit one hour later. As usual there was no R/T contact, and I received a green clearance by signal lamp to land. There was no wind. The wind sock hung limply downwards, so I made my approach using the direction of the 'landing T' displayed, and touched down and opened dive breaks to reduce the landing run. Just at that precise moment a four-engined Liberator on its take-off run came hurtling along on another runway, crossing centrally at roughly 90° to my landing run. Fortunately, he crossed over the intersection ahead of me by three or four seconds. I was pretty annoyed and shocked!

When I booked in at the watch office I asked why the Liberator had been given clearance to take off against an aircraft landing. The answer was completely negative. 'That's OK we use any runway here, a miss-is-as-good-as-a-mile syndrome.'

I was taken into the 'all ranks' dining hall and had a good lunch, nothing spared. A complete, empty dance bandstand was at one end, which seemed out of place way out in the blue with not a female in sight for some 200 miles, and asked the question... 'Sure, we fly nurses in when we have a dance!' was the reply. The USAAF was some air force – all pilots were commissioned with top pay and girls were flown in to keep everyone happy – but I did not think much about their airfield flight control! Later in the afternoon I returned with Lt. McFayden to Amarda Road and unfolded the story to my friends what we were missing in the mess hall.

Routine flying of our Vengeances continued on the TT Flight. The last flight I had with my navigator, Doug Terry, was to the US airbase in Dacca when we flew our chief engineering officer in for one of his meetings. Eventually we lost Sgts. Terry and Skidmore when a posting came through for them to use their qualifications more fully, and eventually they were on their way to a new location. We were sorry to see them leave, but it was all quite understandable. Members of the ground staff filled in for streaming the drogues and seemed to be quite keen to get involved with the flying.

Trips into Calcutta came up from time to time. Often passengers would sit on their own luggage and would compete for a lift into Alipore airfield or Dum Dum airport.

As we settled into the routine of the TT Flight, I was pleased to find that nearly ninety per cent of my flights were for communications and carrying passengers. It should be appreciated that at this time in India, available aircraft suitable for carrying up to three passengers or crew on short journeys were few, which resulted in a fairly regular demand from passengers of all persuasions, particularly as transport by other means was difficult and often not even available.

A number of USAAF personnel remained at Amarda Road to service American aircraft and to cover training procedures. They also had several very heavy vehicles which had power winches at the front of the bonnet, one of which suddenly became the basis for a gallant rescue operation. It had sometimes been said that there were more deaths in advanced flying training and general flying situations than in actual combat...

We were standing around our flight office awaiting instructions on the far side of the airfield, when a USAAF Liberator coming in on a long low approach suddenly collided with a Harvard losing height making a steep shorter approach and about to turn into wind. The Harvard collided with the port stabiliser of the Liberator's tail plane. The Harvard managed to make an emergency landing by the side of the main runway. The Liberator, however, was a split second into a major disaster. The nose lifted momentarily – a surge of power followed in attempt to gain control – the nose dropped downwards and crashed into the runway, skidding along and at the same time bursting into flame. Personnel nearby later said they could hear the crew and a few passengers hammering on the side of the aircraft in an attempt to get out. The American driver of one of the heavy vehicles close to the runway leaped into his cab, drove close to the nose of the burning Liberator and somehow threw the hook of the power winch into an opening in the crumpled nose and pulled a chunk of the broken fuselage apart, allowing a small number to escape. Without seeing details of the official USAAF report, we understood six or seven of the crew or passengers perished in the burning crushed fuselage. The driver of the USAAF heavy vehicle was decorated for bravery for helping some crew members to escape from the burning inferno and risking his own life in doing so.

On 1 July a padre, Sqd/Ldr Xavier and helper arrived on the scene at our flight office and required a lift to meet the Bishop of Calcutta, and it was my turn to make the trip. The outward flight was straightforward and within thirty-five minutes I had circled the balloon barrage and landed at Alipore airfield with my passengers. I went off to find some lunch and in due course returned to meet my passengers for the return flight in the afternoon. I booked out and took off with no adverse weather reported. As we climbed towards cruising height, the clouds closed in and a high buffeting wind and thrashing rain hit the aircraft. After several minutes flying blind on instruments we were into some very undesirable flying conditions – I made a snap decision – this flight was not a matter of life and death, and I had two passengers in the back, so I announced to them I was returning to Alipore and I guessed with no R/T connection it was the best thing for all concerned.

We landed once again in Alipore in due course. The watch office was a bit surprised as they had had no indication of bad weather. The aircraft, however, was dripping with water in confirmation of our experience. It was arranged that we would return to the bishop's establishment and stay the night.

That evening some entertainment had been arranged by the bishop for service people in the immediate area, and this included me. A few steps away, soldiers and a few airmen were gathering in a large room, with chairs already laid out. The high spot of the evening was an Indian in western evening dress, who claimed to be a magician and performed some remarkable acts. The one which stands out in my mind defied gravity. I was sitting about fifteen feet from where he was standing on a level floor. He proceeded to erect an upright metal tube support about four feet high, with a small cup-shaped top. Then he summoned a young woman wearing a sari and bade her put her right hand to the right side of her head. Then he faced her towards the audience, and, fluttering his fingers from head to toe, supposedly put her in a trance. He then lifted her apparently stiff body into a horizontal position and rested her right elbow into the cup at the top of the metal tube, and at the same time making small movements of her stiff horizontal body until he found the mysterious, impossible position that allowed her complete body to stay straight out horizontally, with the only support being her elbow, and there she stayed in full view, with no special lighting and in an open room with no stage and nothing between her and the front row of spectators with myself included.

He then waved his arms above and below her horizontal body to show there were no hidden wires – and indeed this was in a large open room in the bishop's establishment, which was not available for any pre-trick equipment to be installed. The magician then lifted the girl to her normal upright position and de-hypnotised her, and she went off to one side of the room.

This performance was virtually at the end of the evening's entertainment, and the bishop then thanked the various people who had taken part and somewhat uncomfortably thanked the magician for his amazing performance, particularly as his visiting card which was being passed around announced he was a magician and necromancer, which of course did not align with Christianity.

The following morning I met my two passengers and made the return flight to Amarda Road in bright sunshine. A day or two later my two colleagues and myself found to our surprise that we were all due for two weeks' leave.

A Journey to Darjeeling

I already had an open invitation to visit Garth Crees' father's tea estate in Darjeeling. My two colleagues decided to take a ride to see the fine scenery in Kashmir.

In due course, with my official rail pass, I arrived at Calcutta Railway Station on the first leg of my journey to the Lopchu Tea Estate, in the foothills of the Himalayan Mountains. The forecourt of Calcutta Station, if one could call it that, was the usual array of individuals and families on the move. The latter would usually be squatting surrounded by small sewing machines, children, pots and pans and at times even livestock. It seemed they were prepared to wait day and night so long as they got on a train.

A seat had been booked with my rail pass, and before long I and my kit (carried by one of the many carriers of luggage who abound in India) was safely installed on the train scheduled to take me to my destination some 300 miles to the north. The coolie had collected his baksheesh after carrying my luggage and was on his way seeking some more baggage to carry.

The train to Darjeeling was no express, but kept moving at a better rate than in my previous experiences of Indian rail travel. Towards the end of the journey the gradient started to increase as we approached the foothills, and we came to a stop. Here the train changed to a special track, where a different locomotive with cogged wheels for climbing very steep gradients took over, and we finally pulled into Darjeeling station.

From this point on, everything was smoothly organised. A driver from the tea estate was there on the platform awaiting my arrival, holding up a notice announcing Lopchu. The driver took me and my luggage in a small Morris car of the day up into the foothills via a steep winding road to the Crees' bungalow. Here the man himself awaited my arrival. (In those days it was surnames only in planters' jargon, but in the friendliest of ways). A 'bungalow' on a tea estate in India is usually quite a large house with a first floor. Mr. Crees' English wife had died some years past, and he was so lonely that he had married a pleasant Nepalese younger women, and he explained this to me openly, and I admired him. She dressed in normal western clothes.

He was pleased to hear about his son Garth, who was a good friend and with whom I had trained in the early stages of our flying course in Southern Rhodesia, and who had given me the introduction to visit the Lopchu Estate. Out in the foothills around the estate, it was indeed another world. The nearest English neighbour on the next estate was some miles away. Horses were used quite a lot for communication. Motor transport was sometimes difficult because of the steep terrain, where engines would overheat quite easily. In fact the 8 hp Morris car which collected me from Darjeeling station apparently stood up to the conditions rather better than most. Along the steep winding road up to the Lopchu Estate, troughs of water were kept filled, specifically for topping up boiling radiators.

The bedroom given me on the first floor had a breathtaking view of the great mountain Kangchenjunga, 28,168 feet high. The large, white peak which glistened in the morning sunshine way above the cloud layer was some fifty miles to the north-west, over the border in Nepal.

Many of the tea pickers were Nepalese women, who carried a basket on their backs and picked the fresh leaves in front of them as they moved along the terraced slopes.

The food in the bungalow was excellent after the mess food at Amarda Road. The climate in the foothills was perfect for growing vegetables in the kitchen garden. The daily menu was just like home in peacetime and was positively English food. I don't remember having a single Indian dish.

One morning, Mr Crees, who had a touch of gout, asked me if I would join his wife Chetti to visit her Buddhist shrine (explaining that he did not interfere with her Buddhist background). I said that I would, and was surprised when she turned up in the front of the bungalow wearing jodhpurs, a white blouse, no hat and riding a frisky white pony. At that point in my life I had never ridden a horse, apart from a ride on a donkey when I was very small, and later a ride on a camel in Regents Park Zoo when I was slightly older. Some way behind, an Indian boy followed on foot, pulling a less frisky brown nag which was to be my mount.

My horse was already saddled, and all I had to do was to get on it, which seemed reasonable. The young boy held the horse steady, but of course I got on like mounting a bicycle, which was wrong, but I made it into the saddle using much more energy than was necessary. Then we set off at a gentle pace with me holding the reins and the stable boy walking along by the horse's head and more or less keeping things under control – and before long I was glad he was there because, looking to my right, there was a sheer drop and we were but a few feet away from the edge. The horse, of course, knew its way around and was completely reliable. We pressed on with Chetti leading the way, finally arriving at her little Buddhist shrine. Pieces of fruit had been laid out as an offering, and a pole with prayer flags waving in the wind which carried her prayers fluttering to heaven – all very peaceable, gentle and harmless, which somehow fitted into the vastness of the great landscape.

Chetti then announced that we would walk back through the trees, and the clever stable boy took both horses back to the bungalow and stables. We then walked away from the horse track and through the wild walnut trees, which seemed to be a shorter distance but was somewhat uneven in places.

A fishing trip was planned one day, and I looked forward to this; it would take place farther down in the valley in a mountain stream. A large hamper was prepared, rods and tackle were made ready and Crees, myself and the driver got into the little Morris and off we went down to the valley. Somewhere in earlier conversation it had come out that the driver was in fact Chetti's brother, and I believe he had been a soldier in a Gurkha regiment fighting the Japanese, and had been wounded and then discharged.

We parked some way from the water and my kindly host took one look at the water and said 'It's no good, there's been a land fall.' The water was not clear, as it should apparently be for fishing in these parts, and was earthy-looking. So we had our lunch – Crees and I sat on folding chairs by the hamper, and the driver according to custom sat some fifteen feet away preparing his own repast, which he cooked on a small fire. All this was a bit strange to me, but not so up in the foothills of the Himalayas, so I took it all in my stride.

A roving English 'tea-type representative' arrived at Lopchu one day riding a horse. He was also involved with other tea estates in the area. I knew absolutely nothing about how the tea trade in the area operated, but he seemed to be well versed in all aspects of life in general, and seemed eager for conversation. He was very interested in flying and almost knew more about aero engines than I did, but he got a bit out of his depth when discussing the Wright Cyclone twin-row radial engine. Apparently the white planters had already formed some kind of a Home Guard and would be ready if the Japs should break through. I felt that perhaps if this did unfortunately come to pass, he would be in for a rude awakening.

One morning I awoke to a lot of shouting on the tea slopes, and it appeared that a bear had suddenly made its presence known, much to the alarm of the arriving tea pickers. The noise generated appeared to have driven the animal off, and I was disappointed that I had not seen the creature. Some years later I looked up the references to the wildlife in those parts and found that the bear would have been a Himalayan bear, which was different to the black sloth bear found more commonly farther south.

After a few days, quite suddenly I was surprised to find I had come out in a rash. In India rashes must be reported at once. *The Doctor Baboo* who was possibly a failed medical student, and who kept an eye on the health of the tea pickers, was summoned and arrived on the scene to inspect my rash. I was consigned to my bed, and in fact felt quite under the weather. Chetti brought me a bowl of chicken soup, which was much appreciated. Very soon an army ambulance arrived, which had a canvas back and a red cross on the side, and had the appearance of something left over from World War I. Mr Crees had possibly experienced a similar situation before, as he had previously made welcome a number of service people, and knew instantly the right procedure.

The army hospital at which I stayed took my full details, so I was logged in officially, and as far as I could see was the only RAF patient on the premises. The nurses were unfortunately all male, but they did a good job. In due course I was told that I had a mild attack of dengue fever, although they did not seem to be completely sure. I was given some horrible medicine referred to by the orderlies as custard oil.

Eventually after about a week or so I was discharged and given an extra two weeks sick leave. This found me in Darjeeling with my kit, amongst a small crowd of soldiers and an RAF tradesman who professed to having been a jeweller before entering the RAF. He was busy collecting gems and uncut stones which he kept in a divisioned box, with all items carefully itemised. Apparently Tibetan traders often brought in gemstones both cut and uncut, into Darjeeling, and if one had the knowledge one could make a good purchase.

I started to amble along the main path in the township with a bearer carrying my kit on his head, without realising exactly where I was, when a voice shouted out to me and I was overjoyed to see it was my friend Crees, standing chatting outside the Planters' Club. 'Come back to Lopchu, Connor boy.' Which I did of course.

Some days later I had lunch with him at the Planters' Club, and I had an opportunity in the township to buy a few small garnets, a moonstone and an opal from a Tibetan wanderer. These were only semi-precious and quite small.

Back on the tea estate Mr Crees showed me how the leaves were graded and dried, and I had an opportunity to send a large parcel of orange pekoe tea back home to my mother and father. Many weeks later I heard from them that they had actually received the parcel intact, which I thought at this time of war was a minor miracle. My parcel might well have been flown back to England as parcel post coming from service personnel. Of course at the time in the UK tea was heavily rationed and in very short supply; orange pekoe is a high quality and I imagine almost unobtainable. The large parcel of tea was a great bonus for them and I was so pleased I was able to send such a gift. Mr Crees arranged the dispatch of the parcel with his other consignments sent via Calcutta.

I was very grateful for the kind hospitality afforded me. Eventually my overall leave plus sick leave ran out and I returned to my friends on the Vengeance flight at Amarda Road at the beginning of March 1944. They were all curious about my somewhat long absence, but it was all official. We exchanged stories and were soon back into our flying routine.

The third navigator, Sgt. Hindel, still remained with us, and he flew with me for two particular trips when we took our chief engineering officer Sqd. Ldr. Middleton to a US airbase for special meetings. For the return trip we had our fuel tanks filled with American 'Lend-Lease' fuel for which I had to sign! In between the passenger flights the occasional target-towing flight came up, with Cpl. Freeman and L.A.C. Boothe streaming the drogue for fighter target practice. Sometimes the live rounds came closer to our aircraft than hitting the drogue, in which case one of the drogue operators would fire a red warning signal towards the oncoming fighters, which when fired from inside the open rear section of our aircraft left me with the momentary impression that we had been hit rather than the drogue.

Back at Amarda Road, there was very little to occupy our minds apart from reading when we were not flying or sitting around in the flight office. When back in our hut, Derek Killey, who had previously acquired a wind-up gramophone, played us some soothing classical music and also some popular songs of the day. One of the latter which still sticks in my mind was a song called 'Gloomy Sunday'. As far as I can remember it had a catchy soulful tune and was sung by Ella Fitzgerald, and the words started with. 'Sunday is gloomy, the hours are numberless...' There was something about this song which was apparently blamed for a bad situation but more about this later.

When things were not too hot, we sometimes amused ourselves playing a rather loose version of badminton. We had a net, a couple of rackets and shuttlecocks. I cannot quite remember how we obtained these, but it all helped to pass the time. One of the very friendly airfield controllers, Dave, the ex-butcher, was a good few years older than we three flying types – fairly portly in physique but surprisingly fast on his feet, gave me many a knockabout with the shuttlecocks and plenty of humour – I will always remember him. With great care when on duty, he would use his signal lamp to give us the green for take-off or land, or red for stop or unsafe to land.

On 26 September our flight commander, F/Lt Porteous, decided we should put on a Vengeance flying display for the rest of the station. The flight of four aircraft would be flown by himself and we three pilots who had completed the dive-bombing course. Porteous was anxious to fly the box of four and perform around the circuit. I had the hated number four position of formatting directly below Porteous.

We took off with a flourish together on the runway in the usual manner, and quickly formed up into the box. We all had a ground-staff passenger and I had Cpl Freeman, one of the star drogue streamers. Not many at Amarda Road had seen the box of four in action, and it made an unusual sight. We whizzed around for a bit and F/Lt Porteous, I thought, felt quite pleased taking the lead in a box of four, but not being practised in the exercise himself as he had never flown a Vengeance before he came to Amarda Road. This I knew, as when he had first arrived on the scene he asked me to take a flight with him and explain a few points about the unusual characteristics of the aircraft.

The formation pressed on, and when still tight up in the box, 'Porty', as he had come to be known, decided to fly closer to the ground without opening the formation out to echelon starboard or something suitable. After having flown over the airfield, Porty continued to lose height to a low level – so low that I was beginning to think that I would have to break away. However, he suddenly levelled out, and being a few feet below his aircraft I was at an exceptionally low level. Fortunately it was a very flat even terrain, with no trees or projections, and my enforced concentration was in overdrive. At last Porty climbed back to a manageable height and we went into echelon starboard and then circled the airfield steeply in line astern, finally landing as a formation in the usual manner. In fact it was a fairly swanky performance and although amongst the flying fraternity not a lot was said, it showed that the Vengeance was a lot more manoeuvrable than thought by many.

Back in our communal hut we had a bearer who arranged our laundry. He also brought us tea every morning which he collected from the cook-house after having walked from his small village some eight or nine miles away beyond the paddy fields. One morning he did not turn up. His excuse was that a leopard had been seen in the area of his village, so he waited until it was safer to take his morning walk.

It appeared also that a white missionary lived in his village, which seemed somewhat strange as nobody seemed to know anything about this person. One weekend Derek Killey, who had acquired this information and I decided to take a long walk out of general interest. Anyway, it was something to break the monotony of the overheated, uninteresting surroundings – parched sun-baked earth and barely a tree in sight.

The walk itself, which crossed some paddy fields, brought home to us what our bearer did every morning to make a living, but to him it was quite a good living as he collected a couple of rupees each week from a number of NCOs. Eventually we located the village, which was enclosed by the usual rough boundary fence to keep out the occasional bear or leopard. We soon found the missionary's hut amongst the native dwellings – his was an extremely small hut which amounted to one tiny room. He had a bed, a small table, the smallest sideboard imaginable and the odd chair. He was very old and frail due to a long life in the tropics. His English wife had been dead for some years, and her photograph was perched in the middle of the sideboard. A crucifix indicating his life's work hung in a prominent position. There had been no formal introduction from our bearer, who did not speak very much English anyway, but he may have mentioned we were coming to see him.

We just somehow arrived, and it seemed that nothing ever surprised him. He did not have much to say, and we found it difficult to make conversation. We left him a few cans of food and departed, feeling that we were almost intruding on his existence. It appeared that he was so old his immediate surroundings were his only interest. (We had previously tried to give our bearer some food, as there had been a bad rice harvest, but we later found it lying about, as he was a strict vegetarian and the cans contained meat in some form).

It appeared that an aged solitary Christian missionary lived in a remote primitive Hindu village without any serious problems. Derek and myself made the return walk without incident and put it all down to broadening our horizons. Amazing how some souls plot their lives!

9 October – Yet another missionary, Rev. A Dontaine, arrived in our Flight Office and needed to be flown into Alipore,

Calcutta. My instructions were to take the flight in Vengeance 134, stay until the 11th, and bring back Squadron Leader Tate in Vengeance 696 – a glorified taxi service in redundant dive-bombers. As far as I can remember, this produced a couple of decent meals in Firpos Restaurant, a trip to the cinema where I saw *King Kong*, which chalked up a minor cinema goer's record by completing a triple viewing of *King Kong* in three continents – once in the UK, once in Bulawayo, and now once in Calcutta.

After my return to base there were a number of passenger flights to Alipore taking in Kanchripara. Two target towing flights were also on the agenda, and some local flying.

1 November gave way to an unusual assignment for me, bordering on a flying circus. It became necessary for a large 'nose wheel' of a Liberator aircraft, plus two senior technicians, to be transported to Dhubalia urgently.

These large four-engined aircraft were used for a number of different purposes, including long-range reconnaissance, bombing, flying VIPs over long distances, (Churchill used one, converted to suit his own requirements, when he flew to Egypt), and, finally, urgent transporting of cargo, including aviation fuel in bulk, when converted into a flying tanker.

It appeared that the only available aircraft suitable for the purpose was a Vultee Vengeance. The rear section was quite spacious, but not quite large enough to completely accommodate the diameter of the nose wheel, so it was wedged in fore and aft and protruded upwards like a large boiled egg. I thought this might upset the flying characteristics of the aircraft, but I was assured by our chief in charge of overall maintenance (who hated flying) that all would be well!

The two technicians piled in each side of the wheel. I taxied out and took off gingerly and flew very sedately. To my surprise, after the one-hour flight we landed without any noticeable problems. The two passengers scrambled out and the nose wheel was extracted. I refuelled and returned to base, knocking five minutes off the flight with a gentle tail wind. I guess that was just about the most unusual flight I had made to date.

On 3 November I had another flight to US airbase Tezgaon with Sergeant Hindel, as navigator, taking passenger Squadron

Leader Middleton for a meeting. Just as we were about to return, a Red Cross/USAAF member hitched a ride to Calcutta, as we were due to over-fly the area. He scrambled into the rear with his baggage, and I landed at Dum Dum Airport without any fuss from the watch office control. There was no R/T connection due to the different frequency, so a green signal lamp had given me permission to land. I taxied around to a convenient point, our passenger climbed out – with engine still running I taxied back to the take-off point, awaited a green signal and returned to base.

7 November – A further flight with Sergeant Hindel came up to collect Squadron Leader Middleton from Tezgaon.

21 November – I had another flight to Alipore/Calcutta and back, and noticed I had another rash. Once again, panic set in for our Medical Officer. Another of the pilots on the TT Flight, W/O Scholes, then flew me back to Alipore/Calcutta for transfer to the RAF Hospital. Here I had a closer expert examination. The problem was always the fear of a smallpox outbreak. I was immediately put into an isolation ward for close observation. In the meantime I heard from my friends at Amarda Road TT Flight that the aircraft in which I had been flown to Calcutta by W/O Scholes had been completely fumigated. However, in due course I was pleased to find that I was not on the point of total disfigurement or sudden death, but it was an attack of Rubella (German measles) which had produced the rash – a mainly childhood infection, but one I had missed – seems I was a late starter at twenty-one years. By now I was well advanced through the malady and getting fed up sitting around the hospital ward.

In the meantime I learned that the other two pilots and myself who had previously passed through the dive bombing course in Peshawar had now obtained a posting away from Amarda Road to a Hurricane conversion unit. I was discharged from hospital and duly arrived at 3 Refresher Flying Unit, Poona on 29 November to fly the Hawker Hurricane, a well known favourite of many RAF pilots.

By now I and my two colleagues had become flight sergeant pilots, which gave us a little more pay and came about on a service-time basis. Gradually we were acquiring more and more experience, but because of the theatre we were in our future commitment was somewhat blurred. Here we were in the process of moving towards another flying conversion, which would probably take us eventually into the Burma campaign, and unknown situations.

In the meantime World War II was continuing in ferocity on all fronts, and already, on 6 June 1944 the Allied tables had turned at last and D-Day had been launched into Europe.

Chapter Eleven
A WING AND A PRAYER

3 RFU Poona was a straightforward conversion unit for flying the famous Hawker Hurricane single-seat fighter. By the end of 1944 however, the Hurricane was beginning to get a bit old in the tooth, but in this part of the world it still had an important part to play as it could land and take-off on fairly short forward airstrips, particularly necessary in Burma. It was also widely used for ground attack in this theatre, rather than higher altitude interception.

Initially we had the usual refresher flying Harvards, being a two-seat trainer where an instructor could take a few hours with pilots about to fly a single-seat aircraft which they had not flown before.

In due course it was time for me to take the first flight in the all-British Hawker Hurricane fighter aircraft powered by a Rolls-Royce Merlin XX – liquid cooled, 1,260 hp engine.

14 December 1944 – Immediately I was impressed by this delightful aeroplane. It was so easy to handle and all the controls were in the right place.

I could not find any nasty characteristics with the version being flown. I could now begin to understand why the term 'Landing a Hurricane on a sixpence' came about. Of course there were a number of variants in the different marks which produced some diverse characteristics. There were the pure fighters with ten and twelve machine guns or a mixture of machine guns and 20-millimetre cannon; Hurricane bombers; Hurricanes with rocket rails; and Hurricanes with two 40-millimetre cannon which could rip open the toughest of ground targets.

We flew all the exercises in fighter mode – aerobatics, low flying, battle formation, tail chase, close formation, low level map

OCA flight

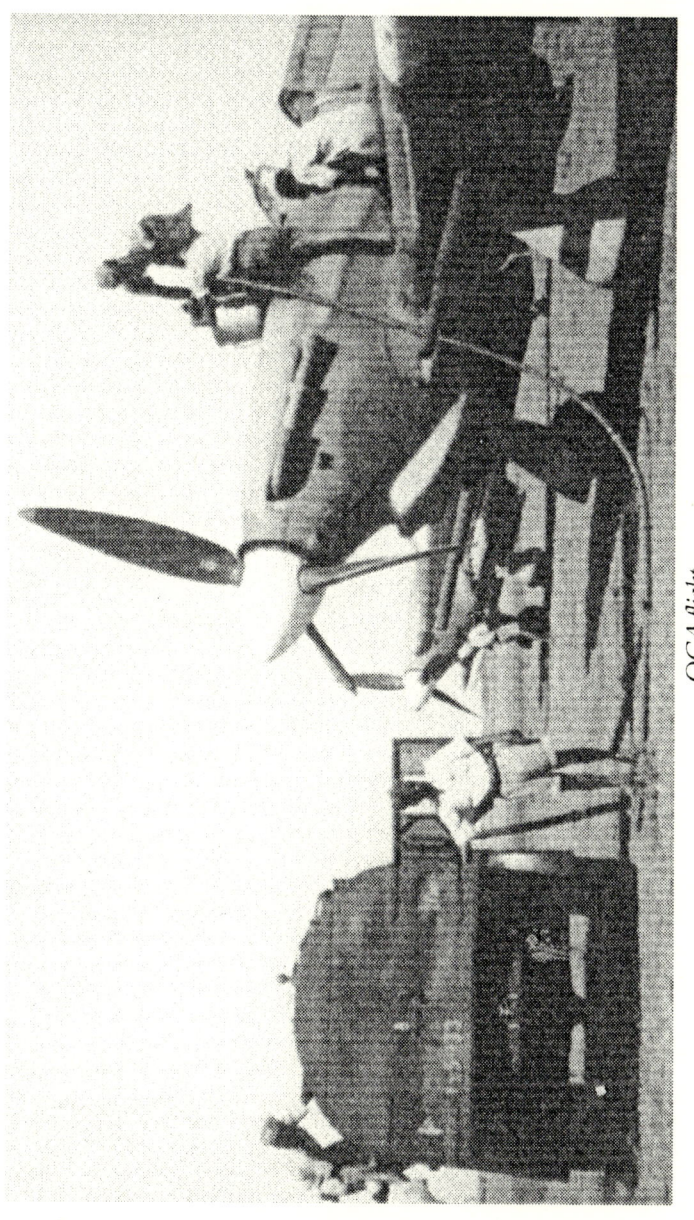

Hawker Hurricane

reading. Two homings and a spin. The latter with no serious hidden difficulties.

The district of Poona close to the air station, from what I can remember, was more village-like and at the time there were no great building structures taking place. There was very little traffic in the immediate area, and one particular road close by was well-dried compressed earth from years of use before the airfield existed. Here one could find a few simple shops with a side-walk made with compressed earth raised up from the roadway, which seemed to be due to a long-standing civilised British influence – much the same as we found in far off Bulawayo, South Rhodesia, where our serious training first commenced.

There was also a European-type park, where some retired English patriotic gentlemen gave us the offer of using their 'sail boats' for a spot of weekend recreation. Amongst the lads there was talk of using these sailing dinghies, visualising something with a keel and healing over in the wind, but of course there was no wind in this sun-bleached inland vista, but we were grateful for the thought. The craft turned out to be typical park row-boats with a handkerchief of a sail amidships, and were sailed on a narrow waterway. A number of us took up the challenge of this daring-do and quickly became becalmed after the merest of zephyrs took us a few yards away from the landing stage. For the rest of the voyage it was oars out, and we did not hang around too long with little of interest in this Empire backwater.

There was not a great deal more to see whilst staying in the area, but some of us found a local Chinese restaurant which we located when off duty. Amongst many dishes produced was an excellent asparagus soup, one of my favourites. Strange that a soup could bring back memories, but this was a particularly good soup.

It was also interesting to note how small Indian communities in outlying areas quickly latched on to any discarded articles somehow left behind by British Forces. On one occasion a path to our billets which skirted a village *dhobi* pond (used for their laundry activities) revealed an unusual canoe tethered to the bank. Upon closer inspection it turned out to be an aircraft drop-tank used for fuel to extend the range of an aircraft, and jettisoned when the tank became empty. These clever villagers had instantly assessed the value of such a find – probably made from specially treated plywood for lightness. A shaped hole had been cut out at the top side which allowed one person to sit in and paddle, probably with their hands.

One lasting memory of Poona was the wailing at night which came from a local jail repeating continuously 'Mahatma Gandhi... Mahatma Ghandi...' – a form of passive resistance from the inmates within. It was a miserable forlorn sound which was not conducive to peaceful sleep.

In due course it was time to complete our conversion on to Hurricanes at a Ground Attack Training Unit located in Ranchi. This involved another train journey from Poona of some 780 miles to the north east in the province of Bihar, arriving 11 March 1945.

13 March – The first flight on this special course was in a Harvard and produced a problem. This was a low level cross-country exercise with an instructor. Very little seemed to tie up with the course I was flying and the map on my knee.

At low level there was not much opportunity to make sense of the few land marks drifting past at the time. Before long the instructor, F/Lt Lister who knew the exercise backwards, twigged that I was having trouble and asked me what course my compass was reading. When I gave him my answer he knew that something was wrong. I was flying what I thought was the correct course, but unfortunately within my own compass was a gaping error in the instrument which required a large correction. He mumbled something about reading the map and that I should have made an allowance for the compass error – which was quite large. I thought this was a bit much at low level – in fact at any level in an area of few obvious landmarks, an inbuilt error of this magnitude was a flying disaster. Eventually, he became more reasonable and throughout the sixty-five minute exercise we compared our compass readings and he gave me the error against his own compass which was accurate. The compass in the aircraft concerned should have been swung on the ground earlier, according to normal procedure, and corrected. The aircraft had probably been used mainly for local flying exercises where the magnetic compass had not been used.

On the same day I then had a sixty-five-minute solo sector reconnaissance, this time in another Hurricane without problems.

The next day there was more trouble in store for me in a Hurricane low level tail chase with some other pilots, and with an instructor leading. I suddenly became aware that my aircraft had developed a bad oil leak. I broke away from the exercise and headed back to base. It was about five or six minutes' flying time back to the airfield and the leak was gradually increasing – it was a harrowing experience. Oil was now spattering my windshield quite heavily and I throttled back in an effort to reduce the flow. It was touch and go whether I would make it. I was at low level – too low to bail out and might have to make a crash landing with all this oil spreading around. I was half mesmerised with the situation – my mouth was dry with concern – would I just make it to the airfield? Every second seemed an age – as I came closer I called up for an emergency landing – with my canopy opened, my goggles down to protect my eyes, I now had to stick my head out sideways as the windshield was now so badly oil-bound – to my great relief the edge of the airfield suddenly came into view, and a glimpse of the wind-sock dangling limply was an added advantage – with wheels and flaps extended, I plonked the aircraft down immediately, as if an unseen hand had helped me. I cut the throttle and switched off the engine. Fortunately a Hurricane does not require a long landing run. A vehicle came out to pick me up and two fitters jumped out to take care of the oily Hurricane. I had some refreshment and a sigh of relief.

A colleague flying immediately behind me in the low level tail chase commented later that as we pulled up over a hump a black puff of smoke blew out from my aircraft. At times like these one can feel *there is more in heaven and earth than we will ever know*. Not a word was said officially about this incident which brings me to the general talk about ground attack training.

There is no doubt that low level flying has few margins of safety if something goes wrong. Before we arrived on this course we heard that an earlier course had produced a run of flying accidents involving both Hurricanes and Beaufighters, which had upset the CO. This was about the time when the song 'Gloomy

Hawker Hurricane

Sunday' was going the rounds, and apparently the CO had commented that every time someone played this record another crash followed. Consequently this song became outlawed at the CO's request, and so it was.

Our course continued with different exercises – cross-country flights, where on one occasion we had low cloud cover over a specific mock target included in the exercise, which had to be realistically aborted. With another I recall an Indian domestic bullock took exception to our low level arrival and departed at an alarming rate, smashing all records for its species. Then followed Hurricane 30° dive-bombing exercises (somewhat less impressive than the Vengeance 90° ability, and obviously less accurate), also 60° dive bombing and cannon straffing had its turn. The term 'rhubarb' was introduced to our vocabulary for exercises seeking out and hunting impromptu targets over an area. Several mock operational sorties to specific places were also included.

Eventually we concluded the ground attack experience and our next duty was a posting which would take us into the Burma campaign.

A train journey of approximately 200 miles took us back to Calcutta. Here we came under control of 35 PDC where we were issued with our jungle tropical clothing – green/long trousers, shirt, soft sun hat and black leather boots with heavy canvas gaiters. The latter being cooler than standard flying boots, and more suitable for a long walk back if we ever made a forced landing. Last but not least, we retained our flying helmet and goggles. Our clothes were devoid of all badges for security reasons, in case we made contact with the enemy.

Details of our travel arrangements to take us into Burma followed. Our accumulated kit acquired in India was left in store for collection (if we were lucky enough to return in one piece). Our minimum kit requirement was kept in a kit-bag.

We would now be issued with Mepacrine tablets – small yellow tablets which had to be taken continuously whilst in Burma to avoid the effects of malaria whilst in a forward battle zone. When one finally returned to India it was necessary to gradually scale down the intake before completely stopping. It was very noticeable that members of the 14th Army having taken

201

Mepacrine for prolonged periods had a yellowish hue to their complexion, which took some time to fade away when they finally withdrew from the area. It was rumoured that prolonged use of Mepacrine could cause cancer, but I have never had confirmation that this is true or false.

5 May 1945 – Our journey took us to Comilla where we were air-lifted by RAF Dakota air transport towards Meiktila. As we flew into Burma, the course being flown took us over some fairly heavy tropical forest and we did not talk too much – our thoughts were not in a light-hearted mood. This terrain brought with it a serious atmosphere… then the jungle was replaced with a more open aspect, and our hearts lifted with it. After a flight of two hours and five minutes we landed in a more open landscape.

Meiktila had not long been won back by the 14th Army and the area was alive with activity. Despite the high-tuned atmosphere, a lighter side crept in when we suddenly saw a small group of army officers who had somehow received a visit from a group of nursing sisters, and together were crammed in several jeeps. The ripple of laughter drifted across to us, when in a somewhat serious mood We heard later that they had also somehow managed to obtain a feast of strawberries. Ah well! Good luck to them we said, the army had earned their strawberries and a visit from some pretty nurses.

Small tents had been erected for incoming RAF pilots awaiting squadron postings. We were given the option of a choice of squadron activity. Having already experienced the vagaries of bomb dropping from fighter-type aircraft (with thoughts about my earlier bombing test-dive in a Vengeance), I chose the more direct approach with rocket and heavy cannon. This produced a posting with some new arrivals to 20 Squadron flying Hurricanes armed with either rocket rails or heavy 40-millimetre cannon.

Whilst in Meiktila it was possible to wander around the immediate area. Close to our tents was a small Burmese pagoda which had earlier received an attack by Army flame-throwers to dislodge a Japanese officer with sword and cannon within. The whole thing, including the occupant was a burnt-out shell.

Meiktila lake close by had been poisoned by the enemy and the water could not be used. Additionally corpses from the recent vicious battle had surfaced to add to the pollution. Supplies of fresh water were being flown in by RAF transport aircraft.

Eventually the small group of pilots allotted to 20 Squadron, including myself, were all installed as passengers in a series of supply trucks with Indian Army drivers en route to Toungoo, where hopefully we would find our squadron. We were each supplied with a Sten gun, which had the appearance of having been made from a piece of an old iron bedstead, together with a clip of ammunition. Apparently there was a shortage of revolvers, which were more convenient to carry in a cockpit, but in actual use at close quarters, a Sten gun would be more devastating. The overall Burma experience to date had a marked sobering effect upon us all.

Our convoy assembled and as we rolled out of Meiktila a Gurkha military policeman directed the line of vehicles on to a track which should take us some 135 miles southward to Toungoo. In my truck I travelled in virtual silence, apart from the noise of the vehicle travelling over rough ground. My driver did not speak the usual Urdu, of which I had a smattering, but Tamil (a language used in Southern India), so we were mostly down to sign language and grunts.

The convoy travelled in open formation, with the dust of the forward vehicle visible ahead, and the following vehicle at the same distance behind. We travelled over a dried-up stream, and suddenly an Indian Army officer riding a motor-cycle arrived at full speed, turning each vehicle back towards Meiktila as we were on the wrong track, and presumably heading for trouble. In due course we arrived back to the point where the error had begun and the whole convoy set off again on the correct route.

After an hour or so, the convoy came to rest by two abandoned Burmese huts on stilts. We also found to our delight that a brew-up of tea was being prepared in a large metal container over a fire by a British soldier. This all seemed to come about by special convoy signs understood by drivers. The soldier jovially announced that he came from Dagenham, and we all rummaged around for our tin mugs and agreed that the refreshment would be a life saver. We were thankful for the British Army's skill in rough travelling techniques. The soldier proceeded with confidence and explained that the twig floating on the top of the brew attracted unwanted foreign bodies – this knowledge I had already acquired from my Boy Scout days some years previously. The rough Burma experience had some similarities to scouting.

Whilst we were standing around waiting for tea, I thought I would take a look inside one of the huts on stilts. I clambered up the native-built entry ladder, and peered inside. It looked as though the occupants had left in a hurry. A few clay pots were lying indiscriminately sideways on the floor and nothing else was visible. I decided not to enter in case of a booby-trap. I came down the ladder for my mug of tea.

A lake was close by on the other side of the road, and with several of my new-found friends I sat on the bank surveying the scenery. No doubt the lake overflowed regularly at the height of the rainy season – hence the huts on stilts close by, apart from visits by wild creatures!

One of our number suddenly decided to try out his Sten gun with the single shot button, and the resulting sound appeared to echo around for miles, leading us to conclude that this was not a very good idea.

The convoy pressed on and eventually, after a long, tiring journey, we arrived at 20 Squadron's airstrip. Our kit was offloaded and we found a tent with the CO, Squadron Leader Millar, full-length at rest. Each reported to him upon arrival. We were allotted a tent and told to await instructions. The aircraft were parked nearby.

The action one could expect in this kind of war was ground attack in support of the army. As all aircraft were grounded at this juncture, it appeared that in this area the army was on top of things. In any case new arrivals would at first receive some kind of introduction.

It was a strange reception in this tiring tropical atmosphere, with nothing happening after the long journey. All appeared to be tent-bound, and apart from water, we got nothing in the way of refreshment until the following morning.

We learnt a few days later that some time before we arrived, a lone Japanese soldier had crept on to the airstrip at night, sat beneath a Hurricane aircraft holding a grenade and succeeded in blowing himself up, but only making a small hole in the fuselage, which was easily repaired. A crazy way to throw away one's life!

One morning it was announced that the squadron was returning to Meiktila. The new boys would have to return by truck in the same way as we had come. Our return to the airstrip close to Meiktila was uneventful and we were soon installed once again in our tents.

Quite suddenly the CO and his number two unexpectedly took off to make a ground attack on a target which was apparently creating some resistance to the British Army's advance in one sector. Hurricanes armed with heavy 40-millimetre cannon were used. The two aircraft returned safely, but the pilot flying as number two to the CO found to his surprise upon landing that a single neat hole from a Japanese pot shot had passed through the tail end of his fuselage. This created some amused banter, but in reality it could easily have been much worse.

Our lifestyle under canvas was bearable, but the food was not very satisfying. It included soya bean sausages, more accurately named soya-links, which were somewhat greasy and unpalatable. The word went round that anybody who had kept a blanket, (completely unnecessary at this time of year in the heat) could trade it in to the local villagers for a chicken, which the squadron cook would be pleased to roast. I had retained a spare blanket in my kit, which I immediately passed out for barter. How or when this was done I had no idea, but my chicken arrived roasted and hot soon after – maybe a group barter scheme produced more than one chicken – but I was delighted. It was only a small chicken but the taste after soya-links was a treat beyond words.

Four of us were resting in our tent one mid-morning, writing letters and waiting for something to happen, when out of the corner of my eye I saw a very small silver-coloured snake, about six inches long, making its entry under the tent wall. I had read about the silver krait which was about this size, and that its bite could kill in four minutes – in a startled voice I said aloud 'Look out – snake!' All reflexes were up to standard – the tent emptied in a flash.

Fortunately a longish piece of bamboo was handy and I was

the one who had seen where the snake had come in – the bamboo was long enough for a safe swipe at a distance, and I hit it with an unnecessarily frenzied force. The end of the bamboo had split into pieces and the snake lay stone dead. The smashed corpse was disposed of a good distance away, just in case kraits wriggled around in pairs. The four of us were all on the alert for a period until the 'white hunter' syndrome wore off!

We all now quickly got back into some local flying, and on my second trip, on 14 May 1945, in a change of aircraft, I flew into a most unusual problem. On my take-off run down the airstrip, just prior to lifting off, I noticed that my flying instruments were not reading correctly and my airspeed indicator was wildly fluctuating. I was too far gone to abort my take-off, and as I started to climb away gingerly both needles of the altimeter and air-speed indicator were sweeping back and forth.

I climbed up to about 1,000 feet and started to orbit the airstrip, calling control to make an emergency landing with explanation. I was immediately answered by my flight commander, F/O Johnny Horrocks, offering to come up so that I could formate on him to bring me in to land. I declined his kind offer. I was anxious to get back on terra firma, and replied that I was coming in straight away. In a fleeting thought, I felt that having flown Vultee Vengeances earlier, with various uses of flaps and dive-brakes I could survive a landing in a Hurricane without instruments. I decided to make a precautionary landing flying in very low, and by rough judgement, faster than usual, with wheels down and flaps halfway down, gently lowering the aircraft until I brushed the ground at speed and cut the throttle – it worked! I then had to start braking, as there was not much airstrip left to use. The aircraft objected with a shudder, but I eventually stopped within a few yards of some palms! 'Well done,' came the voice of Johnny Horrocks into my headset – but I thought 'more by luck', or was it that unseen hand that helps in times of stress?

I taxied back to dispersal and the onlookers immediately looked to see if the pitot tube cover had been left on, which is tied on for protection when aircraft are parked. But no, this had already been removed before take-off by the ground staff as was the norm, and also in theory the pilot should also check this himself before climbing into the aircraft.

In due course the pitot tube of the aircraft I had flown was closely inspected, and the culprit was revealed – a hornet species of insect had crawled into the pilot head, probably at night, and extruded a gummy mush. This played havoc with the passage of air flow and air pressure through the instrument, which normally produces vital air-speed and altitude readings via the air-speed indicator and the altimeter. In future all pitot tube covers would be bound on much more tightly when the aircraft were parked, thus preventing further visits by flying insects. Just another hazard which had to be overcome in this tropical environment which could cause a serious accident.

After I had made a total of just five flights from this airstrip, 20 squadron received orders to pull out completely to re-equip. One group of pilots, including myself, flew out of Meiktila in an RAF Dakota on 9 June 1944 and arrived in Camilla. The following day we flew by Commando aircraft to Barrackpore, Calcutta.

There we had some leave as a group, staying in fairly comfortable local accommodation organised by RAF authorities in the area. Calcutta did not offer a great deal on which to spend one's leave for more than a few days. Boredom would soon set in. This was alleviated to a degree by the occasional game of chess with another pilot, Dave Comber, who produced a pocket chess set. A visit to the Hog Market, which was an assortment of stalls selling all manner of goods, was another diversion. You could buy handmade suitcases, and even gents' jackets which could be made to measure in hours rather than days. A trip to the cinema was another option. Eventually it was time for us to join our squadron in Madras, and we then travelled by train to St Thomas's Mount airfield, arriving on 12 July 1945. Another long tiring journey of some 900 miles.

St Thomas's Mount had a small chapel at the top. Several of us climbed the hill, and the nuns within greeted us and showed us around. They pointed out the small cavity in the rock through which the sun shone brightly and where St Thomas had had some kind of vision. The airfield was close by and the chapel was virtually on our circuit.

We continued flying our Hurricanes on local exercises to

maintain our ability. Then we became aware that some naval Wrens were billeted a short distance down the road from our airfield.

From the time we had left the UK, life had been virtually devoid of female company. Training and flying military aircraft was an absorbing business. To date our activities had mainly been in far-flung areas away from normal existence. Suddenly the thought of girls, girls, girls had come to the fore. Funny how our Hurricane exercises seemed to fly in the direction of the Wrens' quarters! Eventually a dance was arranged to take place at the St Thomas's Mount mess hall. The Wrens were invited and they accepted. These young women arrived in a coach and were chaperoned by older and higher-ranked Wrens. One could say the dance was quite formal. I managed to dance several times using a somewhat out-of-practice technique with one particular Wren, and even succeeded in inviting her out to lunch at a suitable time. At the end of the dance the girls were all rounded up and filed back into the coach. This whole affair would not be recognised today, or even back in the UK during the war, but there it was – overseas service in India.

Madras

I had planned lunch in a Chinese restaurant not far from our quarters. The Wren turned up punctually in a rickshaw pulled by the usual native rickshaw coolie at the gates of our RAF quarters – the Wrens' quarters were farthest away from the built-up area, and the meeting arrangement was at her request. I was on cue awaiting her arrival with enthusiasm and joined her in the rickshaw. We set off at a surprisingly good rate of knots, and in no time at all I paid off the coolie and we entered the very oriental Chinese restaurant. (Some Chinese restaurants in India seemed to be more heavily imbued with the Orient than others I had visited). From what I can remember the food was up to expectations. The Wren was a pleasant girl named Lynn and talked the whole time about her earlier duties in Trincomalee, in what was then Ceylon, and her Australian boyfriend in the Fleet Air Arm to whom she was virtually engaged. Oh boy! This was the cold shoulder, and I was the meal ticket. In due course we finished our meal and returned by rickshaw the way we had come. Again she insisted on returning to her quarters unaccompanied, due to regulations, so I paid off the rickshaw coolie to complete her short journey, and that was that.

We continued flying in the area, and before long I started to feel one degree under, although I did not report sick. I put it down to the climate. Then on 27 August it was time for 20 Squadron to move up to AFTU Amarda Road to convert on to a new aircraft. Here I would be returning to an air station where I had previously spent ten months flying Vengeances.

The 20 Squadron move was carefully planned and on this occasion all the new boys had an aircraft to fly. We flew in flights of three aircraft with F/O John Horrocks leading my flight. We flew the move in four hops. The first leg was from St. Thomas's Mount to Ganavaram – this was a long leg – flying time ninety minutes – and here I held off a bit high and my landing was not up to standard, safe but a bit heavy. Perhaps it was because I was a bit off-colour.

Then came news of a disaster. One of my friends amongst the new boys, Sandy Lindsey, a reliable Scot, came up to me and unfolded the tragedy he had just experienced. He had flown with the CO's flight of three aircraft. Instead of following the coast, the CO had decided to take a shorter straight course which, because the coastline wavered inwards, took them out to sea by some twenty-five miles from land at the widest point. Unfortunately they flew into some heavy cloud, which according to Sandy was too dense to hold the formation. This was big trouble; Sandy himself wisely opened his canopy in case of ditching or bailing out, but in the confusion his map blew out of the cockpit. Without a map, he turned acutely towards the coast, found it, and followed it until he saw the airstrip and some Hurricanes already parked. The other pilot in the formation never made it. We assumed that having lost his bearing he ran out of fuel and went down in the sea. Unfortunately, not being kitted out for flying over the sea we only carried a parachute, without an inflatable dinghy. No doubt at some future point the CO would have to make out his report, which would be covered by official procedure for contacting the next of kin etc.

At this point it was necessary to press on with the squadron move. From Ganavaram we flew to Vizag – flying time sixty minutes. The third leg was Vizag to Cuttack, another long leg – flying time ninety minutes. The final leg was shorter, flying from Cuttack to Amarda Road – flying time forty minutes. This completed the move without further trouble, arriving 27 August 1945.

The following two days we flew around the immediate area, maintaining our ability. After the second flight of one hour, I was not feeling at all well and reported sick. My tropical stomach was in a bad way, and the squadron medical officer sent me to the No. 9 RAF Hospital in Calcutta for a full check-up.

Here the chief medical officer at the time was a Wing Commander Robson, who specialised in maintaining the health of RAF aircrew. He was an exceptional MO, and thorough in his diagnosis. (It was revealed by an orderly that before W/C Robson entered the RAF he had had an expensive private practice in Wimpole Street in London – so we were getting the best possible medical attention). I was eventually advised that I had tropical sprue and was treated with May & Baker's specialised drugs. The nursing in hospital was superb, with RAF nurses attending us night and day.

The bed next to me held another young pilot with a similar condition, and we compared notes on our progress and joked about some of Wing Commander Robson's investigatory techniques, which included turning us upside down over his shoulder.

It was not long before we were aware that a number of British prisoners of war (recently released from the clutches of the Japanese after British forces had finally and victoriously overrun the enemy positions) arrived at the far end of our ward. They were immediately and expertly subjected to the full and necessary investigation by W/C Robson and medication was speedily arranged. The soothing effect of the charm of the British nurses soon became apparent, but many of these poor fellows would need months of recuperation to bring them back to a normal civilised existence. One particular ex-prisoner had forgotten how to use a knife and fork and had been subjected to some particularly brutal treatment. Just before being rescued he had been held, cramped up in a small cage-like structure where he could barely move. The nurses worked on him ceaselessly under W/C Robson's directions, and although his physical and medical condition was bad, whilst I was still in hospital he started to show signs of recovery.

Some kind English ladies from the immediate area provided us with some craft-type equipment and materials to while away the long hours of recuperation. I chose to do some leather work, and covered my flying log book in a very durable leather cover with a cowboy-type fringe. Additionally I made a leather note case for correspondence embossed with the RAF emblem, *per ardua ad astra* with crown and eagle; both are still in place to this day. My stay in hospital was from 6 September until I was finally discharged in Calcutta on 20 October 1945. The return to a temperate climate would complete my treatment. This meant that I would shortly fly home at last, and plans were already in progress. In the meantime I heard that 20 Squadron were completing their conversion on to their new aircraft and were then flying out to Siam (now Thailand). I had no news of what aircraft they had acquired, but it was likely to be one of the later marks of Spitfire specially equipped for close support of the army. The war back home by now was over, but there were some ragged ends still to be cleared up out East.

I was able to visit the Hog Market again in Calcutta before I left the hospital and acquired a rather flash sports coat (made to measure virtually overnight), and also a solid leather suitcase to bring home my small treasures, including a very ornate Chinese bed jacket for my mother.

Chapter Twelve
HOME AND THE FINAL PHASE

At last on Saturday, 20 October 1945, our kit was assembled, and with a small group of medical repats we set forth for the first stage of our journey home – for me after three years and 114 days' overseas service. The starting point was Howrah railway station, Calcutta – dirty as ever and to complete the picture it was drizzling with rain at the tail end of the monsoon season. The same mass of humanity sprawled over the platforms – coolies carrying baggage on their heads weaved in and out of whole family parties squatting on the floor. Some Indian Sikh troops grouped together surrounded their mound of kit for safety. Spencer's tea boys, with their regulation company turban-type head-dress, plied back and forth with their cry of 'Tea and toast.' (Amazingly this Spencer's refreshment could be found on any prominent railway station at the time.) Fruit wallahs with their full baskets of fruits paced up and down, but on this trip no one in our party homeward bound would dare risk a purchase of unwashed fruit in case of an attack of gippy tummy. A grubby-looking *char wallah* with his battered steaming kettle of hot tea in competition with the Spencer's tea boys made his appearance and shouted his arrival. The abundance of cigarettes and tobacco for sale was another feature of the Indian scene at the time, both cheap native product and well known brands. As usual, bed rolls, brass cooking pots and cages of pet animals surrounded family groups on the move. A local policeman could be seen strolling across the forecourt – bright red turban, khaki uniform and baton under his arm ready for immediate use.

Eventually, sitting in a wooden third class compartment with the rest of the party we moved off at 3.10 p.m. on the first stage of our journey homewards. The thought of returning home overrode the quality of the travelling conditions. The last view of

Howrah Bridge appeared through a haze of still driving rain. A landscape of sago palms and paddy fields opened out, then a large Bengali house followed by a dirty little settlement or village came into view with the rice nearly ready for harvest – I wondered to myself if it would get reaped in time – now some more paddy, followed by banana trees and coconut palms – every shade of green imaginable.

Our first stop came into view – a place unmarked on most maps called Andul – even thicker masses of palms – irrigation canals and native boats – the train rolled on – filthy swampy looking paddy – some sleepy domestic bullocks chewing away as usual, awaiting to be harnessed to their carts.

My companions in this uncomfortable third class carriage had no grumbles on this trip. We would put up with anything provided we kept going forward, every hour being an hour closer to our homecoming. By 4.05 p.m. the sun had broken through the low stratus cloud which brightened the view and the train passed over a bridge which I recognised as a pinpoint when flying into Calcutta last year. The paddy fields were very flooded at this point. Our second stop was Machada – a typical Bengali jungley wallah's station – small boys yelling their heads off 'peanut wallah' – almost at the same time another *char wallah* arrived on the scene – then a deformed cripple cried for his baksheesh – so much of this that it becomes a backdrop, and sometimes this is a planned condition. We moved on, and to add to the atmosphere we saw a flock of greedy vultures surrounding and tearing apart a carcass of a dead animal, probably a cow.

Our third stop was at Kargpur at 5.35 p.m. It was one of the largest junctions in India. Here we found a Free HM Forces Canteen on the platform – a mad scramble developed. The ever-so-chummy Anglo-Indian train driver leaned out of his cab and, surprisingly, in an almost Indian-cockney accent said 'We're stopping twenty minutes here mate.' We found some brief refreshment. We moved off, and a large, well laid out Anglo-Indian workers' housing estate came into view. The train rolled on – now a native settlement, then rows of grubby hut-like buildings, then some cleaner versions, followed closely by a factory chimney – I had flown over this area on numerous occasions, but it looked somewhat different from 3,000 feet. Still low stratus cloud and the rain started to drizzle again – no palms now but ordinary looking trees – more rows of workers' houses and then four sago palms close up to the track. Still plenty of water about and more paddy – very flat landscape. By 6.20 p.m. the light was gradually fading – the monotonous motion of the train, with no clear view to see in the half-light, took over. Eventually at 9.30 p.m. we arrived at Dalbhumgarh – no organisation whatsoever. This was our first positive staging post and it appeared to be a complete shambles. Nobody seemed to be interested in a group of medical repats!

It was not until three days later that we left this depressing staging post and weighed in officially at the first class transit camp at Chakulia – this was an extremely well organised camp run by the Army. Every requirement was catered for – good billets, bed sheets and mosquito nets, good food with utensils in a pleasantly arranged dining hall. Here we stayed until 1 November. This appeared to be a part of the peacetime Indian Army scene as portrayed in many old records and story books. However, with the onslaught of World War II all this style had crumbled away, but suddenly at this point it had re-emerged. After tiffin time came a period of rest. It was very easy to slip back into this previous mode of existence, when one was surrounded by complete afternoon quietness. The warm fresh air and the comfort of an easy chair on a veranda completed the experience. From this point, the empty road ran away like a black snake to who knows where. The silence was temporarily broken by the solitary purr of a dispatch-rider on his motorcycle, but stillness quickly returned.

I had just about got back to my restful state of mind when things started to point towards a positive homeward journey. The noise of several truckloads of 'Blighty boys' arrived on the scene. Animated voices mingled with the sound of the transport completely blew away any tranquillity, and the thought of going home excitedly brought me back down to earth.

Bright and early on the following morning 2 November, at 05.40 hrs, my group assembled in the transit shed ready to board Dakota 239 to be flown by F/Lt Hapgood. Seating arrangements on the aircraft were primitive, to say the least. Our kit was stacked down the centre of the fuselage, and we sat each side facing inwards with our backs against the fuselage side in single lines, on looped canvas seating. If one twisted around sideways a view could be seen through the fuselage windows. We had no safety straps or belts. Take-off Chakulia: 06.15 hrs. Landed – Palam airport (Delhi) 10.55 hrs.

Take-off – Palam: 11.55 hrs. The course took us over the Sind Desert – we landed Mauripur (Karachi) 15.40 hrs. There we stayed awaiting a fresh aircraft.

6 November, Dakota 487 – pilot: F/Lt Kipper. Take-off Mauripur 06.15 hrs. Landed – Sharjah (Saudi Arabia) 10.40 hrs.

Take-off Sharjah 12.30 hrs. Landed – Bahrain 14.50 hrs.

Take-off Bahrain 16.05 hrs. Landed – Habbanyia 20.15 hrs.

7 November, Dakota 487 – pilot: F/Lt Kipper, take-off Habbanyia 16.20 hrs. Landed – Lydda 19.45 hrs.

8 November, Dakota 487 – pilot F/Lt Le Huray. Take-off Lydda 16.10 hrs. Landed El Adam 20.20 hrs.

9 November, Dakota 487 – pilot F/Lt Le Huray. Take-off El Adam 08.15 hrs. Landed Catania (Sicily) 12.50 hrs.

10 November, Dakota 487 – pilot F/Lt Le Huray. Take-off Catania 06.15 hrs Landed Elmas (Sardinia) 09.25 hrs. Take-off Elmas 11.20 hrs Landed Bordeaux 16.40 hrs.

11 November, take-off Bordeaux 09.10 hrs. Landed Membury 12.10 hrs. At last we had arrived safely back in the UK, and booked into the reception centre. A chilly wet November day was the greeting. My accommodation amounted to a damp room in a hut with dampish blankets. I went straight down with a flu type cold – I promptly reported sick and was put straight to bed in the sick-quarters and dosed with M&B tablets, administered by a WAAF nurse. I believe I missed pneumonia by a whisker.

Some sick leave followed and I arrived home to my parents' house in Barking with all my friends still away in the forces. My parents were both surprised and did not expect to see me so soon, but were pleased I was still alive. They obviously had a bad time in the blitz and had the roof of the house blown off once. When my mother saw the sports coat I had acquired in the Hog Market in Calcutta, she felt it was a bit too bright which was somehow the combination of the tropics and an Indian tailor, and made me look like Max Miller (a loud bawdy comedian of the time). With this motherly observation, I did not wear the offending garment at all, for fear of giving the wrong impression. Having been away from the UK for so long, I had lost my dress sense, and did not wish to drive away any possible girlfriend who might come my way! I am not too sure what she thought about the Chinese bed jacket with its heavily embroidered Chinese design on the back, but she showed it to her friends who regarded it as a rare collector's piece.

With all my friends still away in the forces I decided to visit the Lyceum in town, where young males mostly in uniform met girls and danced to a live orchestra. I was without a female partner, and after a young woman, whose husband had been killed in the war, suddenly sat on my lap without invitation, I decided I was not ready for matrimony quite yet, but did not object to her friendliness.

Still looking for some entertainment whilst on my repatriation leave, I decided to visit some local venues where people of my own age group were likely to assemble, and in December 1945, just before Christmas at a dance in Ilford Town Hall, I met dearest Joan Ellis, the girl I would eventually marry.

In due course, after visiting the RAF Stanmore office for further instructions, I was asked what aircraft I had flown. When it emerged I had flown Vultee Vengeances, this information fitted an immediate requirement and I received a posting to 577 Squadron in Atcham, near Shrewsbury, involved with army cooperation training of AA gunners. The war was over but training exercises never stop. This amounted to a continuous requirement for flying activities which included streaming targets, radar cooperation, visual cooperation and communication flights to surrounding airfields.

Whilst the squadron was at Atcham I was able to get home almost every weekend to see my girlfriend, but it required a late train journey back to Atcham. After the train journey to Shrewsbury it was possible to get a lift in an Army lorry which always met the train for some reason, and which dropped me off along the perimeter of the deer park adjacent to our airfield. This involved a longish walk along the path across the deer park, which led to a footbridge over a stream and eventually to our aircrew Nissen-hut. Usually I arrived back in the early hours of Monday morning, and on one occasion, during some heavy wet weather the stream had broken its banks and the footbridge was several inches under water. There was nothing for it but off with shoes and socks and paddle back to base, and the water was ice-cold, but I thought it worth it to see my love – such is life! The following morning flying commenced quite early, weather permitting, and this meant an early breakfast ready for a possible first flight. It seemed to me that the CO always picked on those who went off for the weekend to get the early flights.

On one occasion I was indebted to a member of the ground staff who was standing by the starboard wing-tip of my Vengeance. He was truly alert whilst I was running up the engine on a pre-flight check before take-off. As I opened the throttle fully to check the instruments he suddenly waved his arms quickly to switch off. He was doing his job properly, and from his position he could see that flames were licking around the inside of the cowling of the radial engine, as the exhaust stub had broken away. Flame is sometimes visible leaving the exhaust outside the engine at full power, but with a broken exhaust stub the flame had no proper outlet, and on take-off at full throttle flame spreading beneath the cowling around the engine could spell disaster. This happened some months before it was time for me to be demobilised from the service. Truly, this man probably saved my life, but the whole thing at the time was so casual that only years later have I pondered this near miss of a disaster, and thought how grateful I should have been for this heaven-sent providence, and I did not even know his name!

In April 1946, to the joy of all pilots, we received a delivery of five Mark 16 Spitfires with Packard-Merlin Engines, clipped wings and a five-bladed propeller for low-level flying, with roughly 50 per cent more power than the Battle of Britain Spitfires. These were powerful beasts and only needed plus four boost for take-off, against a maximum power available of plus seven boost at one's fingertip. This meant that all pilots had at least two types of aircraft to fly for different exercises. There were also twin-engined Air Speed Oxfords for those pilots who had qualified on twins in their previous training. In my case I now had two strings to my bow and continued to fly the Vultee Vengeances and now these superb new Mark 16 Spitfires for our range of activities.

By the end of the month 577 Squadron's base had moved to Hawarden, but our flying programme continued as before, covering exactly the same overall activity, the only difference being a longer journey for me getting home at the weekend.

Before I finally left the service I flew the Mark 16 Spitfire just thirteen times, and on 6 June 1946 sadly flew one of the last Vultee Vengeances No. 428 into a small airfield in Castle Bromwich, barely large enough to make a landing, where the plane was to be dismantled for scrap. The latter was my very last flight in the RAF.

Printed in the United Kingdom
by Lightning Source UK Ltd.
114004UKS00001BA/4-21